Bleeding for Ghosts

For my wife,

Who saw what I was building before I
had words for it.

Who lived much of this story before it
became a book.

Who believed in me without hesitation
or doubt.

For my children,

I carried what I carried so you wouldn't
have to,

and I would do it all again because

my love for you has no limits.

I hope you give the gift of intentional
living to

your own children and their children
later.

Preface: Why This Book Exists

This is not a technical book about personal finance. It's a book about identity in the space of personal finance.

Where my identity was shaped

I grew up poor. Not in the abstract sense and not in a way that invites comparison, but poor by measured economic standards. We qualified for free lunches. We relied on government assistance programs. We lived in a house that was small, worn, and patched together in ways that made sense when money was always the constraint. Work was constant and money was scarce. Emergencies were feared and real progress never seemed to arrive.

I clearly remember standing in line with my grandmother to pick up our free block of cheese at the community center in the town where we lived. I was too young to be aware of any sense of shame that standing in that line may bring, and my grandmother did not give off any feeling that shame was involved. She was not embarrassed, not proud, just there. I was thrilled. If you had the opportunity to taste the government cheese in the 80's that was given away as a result of a massive dairy surplus during that time, you know well why I was so happy. It was delicious! I had no insight into any income qualifications to receive the free cheese; I guess I just thought anyone could stop and get some. Again, I didn't know we were poor.

What I didn't know then was that environments teach long before they explain. No one sat me down and taught me beliefs about money, work, or safety. I absorbed lessons instead. I learned that exhaustion meant responsibility; that fixing things by yourself, no matter how temporary the fix, was virtuous; that asking for help wasn't modeled; that stability was something you chased, but not something you achieved.

Those lessons followed me into adulthood. They followed me through education, career advancement, marriages, parenthood, leadership, and high income. They followed me into debt that didn't look reckless on the surface, but quietly erased margin before I knew what margin even was. They followed me into a life that looked successful from the outside but felt fragile from the inside.

For a long time, I thought the problem was math. If I just earned more. If I just

optimized better. If I just worked harder.
But math was never the point; behavior was.

I realized this as soon as I got into debt
during my first marriage. If personal finance
were only math, very few people would
struggle with it. Budget calculations aren't
complicated. Revenue minus expenses
equals margin. The formula is simple, but
people don't fail at the formula; they fail at
the execution.

A lot of my early debt came from
impatience. From wanting to look and feel
further along than a young, new
professional reasonably should be. For me,
it was about escaping what I had just started
to get away from as fast and far as possible.
It wasn't just a sprint; it was a sprint that
would grow into a marathon.

Credit cards and other debt seemed like
vehicles that allowed financial capacity we
truly didn't have. The question was never
"Can we afford this purchase?" It was "Can
we afford the payment?" People in debt
often focus heavily on the payment, not the
price. That shift from total cost to monthly
obligation is where behavior overtakes
math. It's how you end up with a lifestyle
that requires your current income just to
maintain, with no flexibility and no room
for disruption.

This pattern became even more pronounced during my second marriage when credit cards were used frequently and with more of a focus on managing the payments, not so much considering the need or price of the purchases. Unfortunately, once I became good at managing the payments through careful budgeting, that approach stuck with me for a long time and lost its urgency.

Some debt may be unavoidable, like medical emergencies, accidents, damage from violent weather, and other circumstances beyond anyone's control and budget. But aside from those scenarios, it is behavior that most often drives us into debt. Not ignorance, not laziness, but behavior that is shaped by something deeper.

The most common misconception people have about money is that they can't effectively manage it on their own. In some cases, they simply don't want to, either because it forces them to face uncomfortable truths about their behaviors, or because the language of finance feels intimidating. More often than not, the issue isn't competence, it's conditioning.

It took me years to see that my relationship with money wasn't about what I knew. It was about what I had learned to believe long before I ever earned a paycheck. I didn't start thinking in terms of having a "nervous system trained in scarcity" during the journey. I couldn't see it then. I was too close. Too busy managing systems and maintaining vigilance to notice that vigilance itself had become the problem. It was only after the debt cleared, after the pace changed, after I finally had space to sit and think that I could see the pattern clearly.

I can't point to a single profound moment when this realization crystallized for me. It seemed to be a thought that developed over time that made me realize in many ways I was on autopilot in how I approached my reaction to money and how I managed it. I had been operating with a nervous system that assumed danger was always imminent, even when it wasn't. That framework had kept me alive in an environment without margin, but it hadn't updated when margin became possible. That's what this book is about.

This book exists because personal finance is not primarily a financial matter; it's a behavioral one. It's shaped by nervous systems trained in scarcity, by identities forged in endurance, and by habits that once made sense, but later became invisible constraints.

I'm not writing this to offer formulas or prescriptions. I'm writing it to name

patterns, especially the ones that feel
normal because they were learned early and
reinforced often.

This book is not a how-to guide.

There are countless resources available to
help you budget, plan, invest, and optimize
your finances. Many of them are excellent,
but this is not one of them. This book does
something different. It identifies a specific
situation, when you are carrying an identity
that no longer serves you. Wearing armor
that is no longer needed. Risking your
health for a threat that no longer exists.
These patterns often develop from long or
intense exposure to financial struggles.

If you're looking for step-by-step
instructions on debt payoff strategies or
investment portfolio allocations, this isn't
the right book. But if you're looking for
language, for a way to name what you've
been living, then this might be exactly what
you need because language matters. Once
something has a name, it becomes visible;
and once it's visible, you can decide whether
it still belongs in your life.

After reading this book, you won't have a
new budget spreadsheet, but you will have
the ability to give a name to your situation.
To actively identify what is happening and

the possible reasons for it. To give yourself permission to stand down. To allow yourself to be vulnerable and honest in the mirror. You'll recognize the difference between surviving and living. Between vigilance and intention. Between the warrior who kept you alive and the keeper who might let you rest with focus and purpose.

If you grew up without margin...

If you equate rest with risk...

If you feel safest when you're exhausted...

If you've ever escaped one form of instability only to recreate it in a more respectable form...

This book is for you.

That last one deserves explanation. Poverty on its own is generally looked down upon in society, but high income is sought after without regard to the margin a person may or may not have. This is the typical misrepresentation of wealth. Society celebrates the six-figure earner without asking what their monthly payments look like. Without asking if they can absorb a disruption. Without asking if they feel safe or have agency over their life. The insight into these questions is usually surprising to us because we judge what we see.

When you trade economic poverty for a high-income, no-margin life, you're simply recreating instability in a more respectable form. The house is bigger. The cars are newer. The job title sounds impressive. But the fragility remains. The vigilance remains. The exhaustion remains.

You're still one disruption away from collapse. You've just raised the floor.

This is a story about money, yes, but more than that, it's a story about identity. About the shift from surviving to stewarding. From pushing forward to holding what matters. From bleeding for the past to protecting the future. I didn't know how to make that shift when I needed it most. I didn't even know how to put my experience into words, so I wrote the book I wish I'd had then.

A note on what's missing:

You won't find detailed budget breakdowns in this book. No line-by-line accounting of what we spent or how we structured our debt payoff. Not because those details don't matter, but because they're not the point.

People can imagine what typical household expenses look like. They can picture what inflation feels like in a larger family. The mechanics of those expenses are available everywhere. What's harder to find, and what this book offers instead, is recognition. The ability to see yourself in a pattern you didn't know had a name.

Why I wrote this:

Living it is probably the strongest argument for being qualified to write this book. I wouldn't trust someone who claimed authority over something they haven't experienced themselves.

But beyond that, I was given the unique opportunity to have considerable time to sit and just think about it all. Not searching for answers or looking for external validation but simply examining and analyzing the story of my life from the perspective of money and behavior. To look back with honest reflection.

From a technical standpoint, I have significant academic and practical experience in finance. I've successfully advised clients on their household finances. I understand the math side of personal finance deeply, and that matters, but you can't only address behavior or math individually. Personal finance is a marriage of both, an intersection of operation and theory.

To effectively write a book like this, I needed to be functionally competent but also bring lived experience. A traditional financial advisor has technical knowledge. A therapist understands behavioral patterns. But few are addressing this in the same space as post-poverty or post-debt identity crisis that occurs when the threat is gone but the posture remains.

That's the space this book occupies. If this book has done its work, then maybe quietly somewhere deep in your own life you'll recognize a tired warrior in you, and you'll know when it's time to stop and how to let yourself do so.

Chapter 1: The House Money Built

I didn't know I was poor then.

I only knew that money felt tight, unpredictable, and heavy like something that had to be handled carefully, quietly, and with constant attention. By the formal definition, we met poverty-level income standards in the United States. We qualified for free school lunches and food assistance programs like food stamps, government surplus food, and healthcare that we know as Medicaid. That context matters, not for sympathy or comparison, but because it shaped what I learned long before anyone ever explained it.

Our house was small, about 950 square feet. A single-story tract home set on a concrete slab, with thin walls covered in cheap wood paneling. There was no basement. No second floor. No extra space. What we had was used carefully and fixed creatively.

When something broke, it didn't get replaced, it got patched. Not repaired by professionals but patched by us. Sometimes with help from a family member or a friend who may or may not have had some knowledge about how to do whatever needed done. Hiring someone cost money we didn't have. Replacing something outright was simply out of our reach, so we learned to live with workarounds. With temporary fixes that became permanent. Function mattered more than finish.

There are several examples that capture this mentality. My grandfather put a hole in our fiberglass garage door when a piece of pipe sticking out of the back of his truck hit it while backing up. It was patched with cardboard and duct tape, and that hole was never fully repaired. Another time, I dropped a bowling ball that I was carrying, for reasons I can't remember today, and it rolled into the hallway wall, denting the thin textured wallboard. That dent just got pushed back out from the other side, then the cracked portions were filled with white toothpaste and painted over. You could always tell something happened there because a proper repair was never done. A tree branch fell on our chain-link fence in the back yard and bent it badly. It was left bent and never repaired or replaced. A window in the front of the house was missing its exterior pane because it had been broken years before, and again, it was never replaced. All of these examples and more remained as-is when the house was sold years later.

Even the carpet in my bedroom came from a garage sale. It wasn't installed properly. There was no pad, no tack strips, and no transition pieces. It was simply laid over the vinyl tile and made to work. Nothing about the house was finished the way you'd see in magazines or model homes. All the carpets were worn from years of use. They were shag, leftover style from the 60's and 70's. The vinyl tiles in the kitchen were cheap and faded. Trim was scuffed and corners were damaged. None of it was meant to impress, it was just meant to hold together good enough.

This wasn't framed as ingenuity or self-reliance; it was pure necessity. That approach became more than a household practice, it became a way of thinking. Problems weren't resolved; they were managed. Weak points weren't rebuilt; they were reinforced just enough to get by. Stability wasn't achieved; it was maintained constantly through vigilance.

New things were the exception in our home.

There were things that were new to us, but almost nothing that was purchased new, especially vehicles. There was never a new car in our driveway. Never one that hadn't belonged to someone else before; and not gently used, either, these were well-used cars. High mileage with visible wear. The

kind of vehicles where you learned their
sounds and quirks because you had to.

The first car I remember from my childhood
was a red Ford Pinto. Very small car. Very
unsafe car. My grandfather was about 6'4"
and over 300 lbs was barely able to fit inside
even with the seat moved all the way back,
but that's all we had. That car constantly
had issues too. I was too young to know
what to look for or listen to, but as I got
older, I understood that my grandfather was
connecting certain sounds and smells with
particular issues. He also had a number of
older pickup trucks over the years with their
own quirks. As I got older, I would learn this
well enough to understand what a coolant
leak looked and smelled like, what a low oil
level sounded like, how to hear the
difference between a starter and a battery
issue, and a handful of other early warning
signs.

These cars came with history. With fixes
already done and fixes still coming. You
paid close attention to how they started in
the winter, and you knew which gas stations
had air compressors for leaky tires. You
learned not to expect reliability, only
manageability.

That environment taught lessons before
words ever did. If you grew up in a house
like that, you may recognize what I'm

describing. Not just the size or the materials, but the logic underneath it. The way scarcity disguises itself as practicality. The way making things last feels responsible, even when it quietly costs you comfort, safety, or health later on.

It's just how things were

This wasn't unique to our household. Poverty was generational in my family. My other grandparents also lived in a similar house in the same small town, with similar workarounds and patched-together solutions. My aunts and uncles weren't any different. Family gatherings meant being around people who all carried the same exhaustion, operated with the same assumptions, and lived with the same constant vigilance around money and work.

No one talked about it because there was never anything new to say. This was just how life was. How everyone's life was. I didn't have an alternative model, and I didn't know anyone who lived differently. The warrior mentality wasn't just something I learned from my parents, it was inherited across generations, normalized across my entire family structure. Breaking that pattern meant imagining a life I'd never seen anyone live.

I guess that's not entirely true, there was
one exception. The father of a childhood
friend seemed to know things about money
that no one in my family understood or at
least didn't have access to. I'd hear him talk
about pensions and investment accounts.
He always paid with cash from a money clip,
which was something I had never seen
before, and he always seemed to have plenty
of money, plenty of time, and plenty of
options.

He had a bigger house that was unique, and
it sat on land that was measured in acres,
not square feet. I noticed all of this and
cataloged it, but I never asked questions. I
didn't have the language for what I was
observing, and we didn't have the
relationship where asking felt possible. The
knowledge was visible but inaccessible. I
could see evidence of a different life, but I
had no way to reach it.

I didn't have a bad childhood, though; as
much as I can remember, I was happy. I
didn't feel deprived, I felt protected. I also
felt optimistic; that someday, my life would
look different than those I grew up around.

My parents, who are really my grandparents
that raised me, worked constantly. Full-time
jobs plus additional part-time work. They
were rarely home when I got back from
school. I'd come home alone and wait. I

would typically just turn the TV on and watch it until my grandmother got home. It wasn't a long time, maybe an hour, and not every day. Her full-time work was shift-work, not 9-5 Monday through Friday. I don't recall any particular feeling about this, but I do think it helped develop my sense of independence in a small way.

What I didn't see was money being discussed calmly. When it came up, it came with tension. Grocery shopping often felt stressful, even though no one explained why. Buying anything new, like furniture, electronics, or a car, felt like a big deal, but I wasn't told what the risk was. I just absorbed the anxiety.

I learned early that work was the answer to everything. More work meant more safety. Tiredness meant responsibility. Exhaustion meant you were doing life correctly. These weren't explicit lessons. No one sat me down and said, "This is how money works." The environment did the teaching.

When I use the word margin, I mean something very simple. Margin is the space between your income and your expenses. Some people describe it as living below your means, and that's accurate, but incomplete. Margin isn't just about frugality, it's about room. Room for error. Room for rest. Room for life to happen without everything falling apart.

In our case, that space was extremely thin. Sometimes it didn't exist at all, and at times, it was negative. When there is no margin, every surprise becomes a threat. Every deviation matters. Every decision carries weight it shouldn't have to carry. That condition teaches you to rely on effort instead of space; and effort, when it's all you have, becomes your substitute for safety.

No one ever told me to be vigilant. No one said, "Always be prepared." No one said, "You can't afford to rest." Those lessons arrived on their own anyway.

When you grow up in an environment where things are patched instead of repaired, where nothing is replaced unless it absolutely has to be, you learn something subtle but powerful; problems don't go away, they're managed temporarily, quietly, and with sustained effort. You learn to live with them, and that's how this lifestyle becomes normalized.

It becomes a way of moving through life.

You learn to scan for risk because surprises are expensive. You learn to stretch resources because running out feels dangerous. You learn that stability doesn't come from margin, it comes from attention and effort. From staying just ahead of the next thing that might break.

Over time, vigilance becomes indistinguishable from responsibility.

The first time I recognized this pattern in myself as an adult was through the budget. I was always extremely focused on the budget. I did not want any surprises. So, during points in my life when it wasn't necessary to obsess over it, I still did. I simply didn't want to feel like I missed anything. But I was managing my life vertically through more work instead of horizontally through more margin. I didn't appreciate that a solid base is wide, not tall.

This is how overwork gets romanticized. Tiredness becomes proof of care. Exhaustion becomes evidence that you're doing the right thing. If you're worn down, at least you're not failing. We hold onto that with a sense of pride because the alternative is scary and maybe even painful.

Rest, in contrast, feels suspicious. So, you keep moving.

This isn't a character flaw, it's an adaptation. Scarcity doesn't just limit options; it trains nervous systems. It rewards constant monitoring. It teaches you to trust effort more than structure, vigilance more than margin, and because it works for a while, it's easy to believe it's the right way to live. The problem isn't that these lessons are wrong, it's that they don't expire on their own. The skills that help you survive in an environment without margins don't automatically update when margins become possible. They linger. They shape choices long after the conditions that required them are gone.

That's how you can leave a small house and still carry it with you. Those lessons worked for a long time; they just weren't meant to run my entire life indefinitely.

There was nothing dramatic about it. No moment where I thought, this is poverty, or this is shaping me. It was simply life. The house didn't feel small to me at the time because it was the only house I knew. The repairs didn't feel improvised because that's how repairs were done. Even the exhaustion didn't feel alarming, it just felt earned. When something is normal long enough, it stops asking questions and starts setting rules.

I didn't learn that money was tight. I learned that money was something you managed around, that you worked around it, you patched around it, you adapted yourself to it; and if something broke you figured it out, not because that was noble, but because there was no alternative.

Looking back, what strikes me most is not what we lacked, but how completely I accepted it as the natural order of things.

Food was never wasted. That rule wasn't spoken, but it was absolute. Plates were finished. Leftovers were eaten whether they were appealing or not. If someone else hadn't finished their meal, it wasn't unusual for it to end up on another plate. Throwing food away felt wrong, almost offensive, because food cost money, and money was never abstract.

I didn't experience this as deprivation. It felt practical, responsible, even virtuous. You didn't waste what you had, because you didn't know when you'd have more. That mindset followed me for decades. Long after food was plentiful, the reflex remained. Eating past fullness. Finishing what was there simply because it was there. Scarcity doesn't leave just because the circumstance changes. It stays in the body.

Only much later did I understand that this wasn't really about food, it was about control. About avoiding waste in a world where nothing felt guaranteed. About proving that I could still make things work.

At the time, this felt like competence. In retrospect, it was rehearsal.

When I was about 14, I wanted a dirtbike. Not a bicycle, but an off-road motorcycle. A few of my friends had them and I really wanted to ride trails with them. There was no way for us to afford to buy a new one, or even a reasonably priced used one. My uncle happened to have one that had been sitting on the side of his garage for some time. It was filthy and old and didn't run. He offered to sell it to us for very little money, but the expectation was that I would have to get it running. There was no money to take it in for repairs.

So, that winter I took the entire bike apart in our garage, leaving no two pieces connected. I had no manual, no YouTube, nothing at all for reference, just a determination to make this thing work so I could ride it. I paid very close attention to the disassembly, although I made no notes at the time. I cleaned and, in some cases, painted every part of the bike, then put it all back together. I replaced the spark plugs and oil and patched the torn seat with duct tape. It worked. When I got it all back together and fluids changed, it ran. I was as happy as a 14-year-old boy could be. It didn't look or perform like my friend's bikes, but I was riding and I was having fun.

That dirt bike represented more than transportation or recreation. It was proof that I could solve problems without external help, that resourcefulness and determination could substitute for money, and that if something was important enough, I could figure it out. These were valuable lessons, and they served me well, but they also reinforced a pattern I wouldn't recognize for decades; that the belief that asking for help was a last resort, that struggle was the price of achievement, and that the right way to approach any challenge was alone, with whatever tools I could scrape together.

Chapter 2: Education as Escape

School was stability

I loved school. That never surprised anyone who knew me. I didn't just appreciate the structure; I genuinely loved learning and the academic environment itself. I liked ideas, questions, and systems. The feeling of understanding something better than I had before.

School was predictable, yes, but more than that, it was engaging. There were rules, expectations, and a clear relationship between effort and outcome. If you studied, you learned, and you did well. It made sense.

For a kid growing up in a house where money felt uncertain and adults were always working, school also offered something rare; progress you could see. Education didn't feel like ambition. It felt like relief. It also felt like a way out, even if I didn't have language for that yet.

It also felt like the answer to something I'd wondered about since childhood, seeing my friend's father who understood money, pensions, investments, always having plenty of cash, and a bigger house in a quieter setting. I didn't know what he knew, but I knew it existed, and education felt like the path to that knowledge.

College was never presented as optional. It was spoken about as the obvious next step, the thing that could create a different life. My family wanted something better for me, and they pushed hard in that direction, even if they didn't fully understand the other lessons I was absorbing along the way.

I didn't understand those lessons then either, but what I did understand was simple; knowledge created distance from uncertainty, credentials created safety, and degrees felt like armor. Those beliefs settled in quietly and stayed.

I started college young. Seventeen. I was a first-generation college student, though I didn't think of it that way at the time. I just knew that no one around me had done this before, and that made it feel serious. I chose nursing because it felt like the best path for what I needed, and it was accessible to me.

Learning on the fly

The first day on campus was overwhelming. I had never been to a college campus before, except to use the library at a local university once or twice. Never for a tour, for orientation, not even to otherwise look around. I showed up to register with no real understanding of what I was walking into. No one had explained how enrollment worked, how to read a course catalog, or what the difference was between a prerequisite and a corequisite.

I didn't even know what a Registrar was or what they did. I didn't know that student enrollment counselors were available. It was all done on paper forms since this was before the internet, so it was a very cumbersome and confusing process. Other students had their parents with them, while I just had myself. The extent of my preparation for enrollment was bringing my high school transcripts, ACT score, and checkbook. I learned that day that I would have to take a math proficiency test, which wasn't a big deal in hindsight. I was always good at math, so I did well on it.

I figured it out as I went.

That pattern would continue to repeat itself. I didn't understand the language or the hidden rules. I watched other students navigate the systems their parents had already explained to them, while I worked backward from confusion to competence. I didn't resent it, it's just what I had to do.

What I did understand clearly and urgently was that education was a way out. That pull had been with me for as long as I could remember. Not ambition in the aspirational sense, but something closer to survival instinct. Poverty was never romantic. It wasn't character-building in a positive sense. It was something I needed and desperately wanted to escape. Nursing felt like the most direct route.

I was raised by my grandparents, my mother's parents. My biological parents were teenagers when I was born, so my grandparents adopted me at six months old. This was never hidden from me, and I always had a relationship with my parents. I also have a brother and sister that were raised by my parents, but I was the only child in the house I grew up in. There was no one else around except my grandparents.

The household was quiet in a particular way that comes from age and exhaustion. My grandparents worked constantly, so I spent a lot of time alone. College didn't feel like freedom; it felt like the first step of a plan that might work. Not because it felt like a calling, but because it was practical. It led directly to employment that paid reliably, it was respected, and it felt solid in a way few other options did.

I worked full-time while also going to school full-time. The local community college made that possible. Tuition was manageable if I stayed disciplined and careful. There wasn't room to drift. Everything had to serve a purpose. I paid for the nursing program from the wages of those jobs. There was no college savings account, no student loans, no dorm living, no meal plans. Those things weren't part of my world, so if I couldn't pay for it as I went, it simply wasn't an option.

The logistics were brutal. I worked night shift at a grocery store and evening shift as an ortho tech at a local hospital. Both were technically part-time jobs, but together they added up to full-time hours or more. I scheduled my jobs around classes and clinicals, and sleep happened in fragments. Exhaustion was constant.

Every week was grueling, although I don't recall ever feeling like I questioned my ability to do it all. I think over time it just was just what it was and my "normal" at the time. That alone probably gave me some self-assurance that I could go on. Behaviors that would be reinforced again and again through practice.

There were a few times I barely made the tuition payment. I'd get to the payment deadline with just enough to cover it, and nothing left over. If something had broken, if my car had failed, if I'd got sick, if any single thing had gone wrong, I'm not sure what would have happened. But nothing did, so I kept going. I was operating with no margin, and still didn't know what margin was.

I remember having to buy gas for my car with the change I collected from around the house because the tuition payment wiped me out. Thankfully gas was cheap back then, less than $1 per gallon, but when you're using change, it still seems expensive. That got me through a couple days until I got paid again from one of the jobs.

The nursing program itself was manageable academically. I didn't struggle with the material. What I struggled with was the sheer volume of things I had to hold together at once. Work, school, clinicals, studying, and keeping some semblance of a life outside of all that.

I knew going in that I didn't feel any real passion for nursing. I chose it because it was practical. There was demand in the field and above-average pay. It was a profession people respected, and I tried to do my best at it anyway.

That's how I approached most things. Even if I wasn't drawn to something, I worked hard to be competent at it. I found some areas more interesting than others, like emergency scenarios that required critical thinking under pressure, but none of them felt like a calling. It felt like a tool, and tools don't need to inspire you, they just need to work.

Out of the frying pan and into the fire

That two-year nursing program mattered more than I understood at the time. It was affordable, accessible, and practical, and I'm not sure what else would have offered a similar return on investment so early in life.

Working full-time while carrying a full course load didn't feel exceptional to me at the time, it felt normal. It was simply what had to be done. I learned early on how to compress sleep, absorb fatigue, and keep moving regardless of how my body felt or what my life looked like outside of work and school. That pattern of making it work, no matter what the cost, didn't start in my career, it started here.

To add to everything else, my parents (grandparents) divorced while I was in college that first time and still living at home. My dad moved out. It was the first major emotional upheaval I'd experienced as an adult, and my response was automatic. Keep moving, don't stop, don't process, just keep going to class, keep working, and keep pushing forward. I didn't realize at the time that this was warrior behavior. Treating an emotional crisis the same way I'd learned to treat a financial crisis, stay in motion. The motion itself became proof that I was okay, that the upheaval hadn't broken me. Looking back, this was an early test that confirmed the pattern, when things fall apart, you don't stop to let yourself feel it, to process it, you just move faster.

I graduated at twenty, got married 3 months later, and became a father at twenty-two. Life accelerated quickly, and I didn't question the pace. Movement had always felt like safety.

The first night home with my newborn son was one of the best moments of my life. I loved being a father immediately and completely. That love was uncomplicated in a way almost nothing else in my life ever had been. That was also the first time I knew that what I needed to do wasn't just for me. I needed to create a shield for my kids between where I started and where they would end up. That was my new priority.

The financial part didn't feel real yet. My wife and I had both just transitioned from non-professional jobs with mediocre wages to RN salaries. It felt like we were making a lot of money, more than either of us had ever seen. We had dual income and stable jobs with benefits. For the first time, money didn't feel tight, it felt liberating.

That sense of security didn't last as long as I thought it would. I was optimistic then, maybe delusionally so. I believed I could make anything work if I tried hard enough, and for a while, that belief held. I didn't stop to ask whether I was building something sustainable or just stacking responsibilities faster than I could process them, and at the time, those felt like the same thing.

I took the first nursing job that was offered to me. It was on a cardiac unit at one of the two major hospitals in our area. It was on night shift where most new graduates typically start. It wasn't a specialty I was particularly drawn to, but that didn't matter. The job served its purpose, it paid well, and it offered stability. It validated the decision to choose practicality over passion.

The job itself wasn't terrible; it was just work. I can't point to a single worst night. There were hard shifts of course, with codes that didn't go well, patients who declined despite everything we did, the particular exhaustion that comes from night shift work, but nothing ever made me think I couldn't do it.

The first in a string of opportunities

What I always knew, even then, was that bedside nursing wasn't going to be my long-term path. Not because I hated it, but because I had never planned for it to be. Nursing was a way out of an economic environment, not a career destination.

Less than a year later, I took a job as a manager for a home health company. This opportunity appeared very unexpectedly after I took care of the company owner's wife during one of my shifts. She had a long list of medications that were complex, overlapping, and easy to get wrong.

There were a lot of medications and some of the dosages and schedules were wrong, and a few meds weren't ordered at all. She told me this happens all the time, every time she comes to the hospital. So, I sat on the side of her bed and went through each of her meds one at a time, making sure I had every detail correct before consulting her doctor for an order update. What caught her attention was that I took the time to include her in the process instead of relying on outdated records and assumptions. It was just her and I, one on one, until it was right. That focus and attention to detail is what she conveyed to her husband.

I met her husband the next night when he came to visit her. We talked about his home health company, and about the quality assurance role. We talked about their need for someone who paid attention to detail and could manage systems. A few weeks later, I interviewed for the job and was hired shortly after. I was so young then, just 21 years old at the time, and not even a year out of college.

Within a few years, I was managing the QA department across five offices with five RNs reporting to me. I had no formal training in management and no real qualifications for the role besides being an RN. I had simply impressed someone at a specific moment, and that opened a door I hadn't known existed. This would reinforce my pattern of always watching for opportunities.

There's a thing called Imposter Syndrome where someone doubts their abilities and gives more credit to luck than skill or knowledge. I felt this often and that theme followed me throughout much of my early career. I've always believed that I could do the work, but I've also felt at times like I was taking advantage of opportunities I wasn't quite prepared for. Sometimes I was more than qualified, while other times I wasn't. Either way, the doubt often remained, but so did the forward motion.

That role exposed me early to leadership, to accountability, and to the idea that advancement was available if you were willing to step out of your comfort zone and grab it. I didn't question whether I wanted that path. I only noticed that it existed and it served my purpose.

A few years later the home health company was bought by a larger chain and eventually those offices were closed. I anticipated this happening and moved into emergency nursing before they closed. This was finally something I was genuinely interested in. It was fast-paced and demanding, and it required competence under pressure. I liked the work, but I still didn't feel called to it. It was something I could do well, and doing things well had always been enough. I stayed in emergency nursing for nearly ten years, but by the end of that decade, something had shifted. Not dramatically, just quietly.

I was competent, certified, and experienced. I could handle the pace, the pressure, and the constant demand for quick decisions under uncertain conditions, but I wasn't engaged anymore.

I wasn't burnt out in the way people usually describe it as being resentful, exhausted, and desperately wanting to leave. I was just going through the motions and that work and that environment just no longer excited me. It no longer seemed very interesting to me. I had become very good at something I had never really cared about as a long-term career path.

Nursing had done exactly what I needed it to do. It had created distance from poverty, and it provided stability. It had given me options, but it had never been my long-term plan.

During my time in the emergency department I earned all the certifications that were offered in my role, including Mobile Intensive Care Unit (MICU), Trauma Nurse Specialist (TNS), Advanced Cardiac Life Support (ACLS), and Pediatric Advanced Life Support (PALS). Some of them were about skill development and some of them were about credibility. Each one came with a modest increase in pay, but more importantly, each one reinforced the same message that advancement came from effort layered on effort. Despite the constant motion, it never felt overwhelming. It felt effective.

For a brief period during this time, I also got my real estate license. I thought supplementing my income that way might help. It didn't take long to realize that sales weren't for me. I've always felt uncomfortable taking money from people, especially if I didn't feel like I'd earned it. I didn't like the pressure either. Not pressure on me, I can handle that, but putting pressure on someone else to close a deal felt wrong.

The real estate detour came through a conversation with a friend that I worked with in the ER. We went through the licensing program together, which ended up being lot of fun. What drew me in, honestly, was the money. The idea that you could earn such a large commission from a single sale felt almost absurd.

I didn't last long in real estate, but the experience wasn't a waste. It taught me how property was valued, bought, and sold. It was also the first time I saw real estate as something that could function as an asset. That property holds its value remarkably well, but it also requires significant time and capital to invest in meaningfully. That insight stayed with me, even after I let the license lapse.

I kept moving.

As my income increased, so did my expectations of what life should look like. Not consciously at first. I didn't suddenly feel entitled to more, I just began to assume that forward motion would eventually translate into relief. That stability would show up if I stayed on the path long enough. It didn't. I consistently made more money than I ever had before, but at the same time, I carried more obligations than I ever had before. Expenses rose quietly, and commitments accumulated, but margin never grew.

I didn't yet have language for lifestyle inflation; I only knew that the math never seemed to catch up to the effort. We were running a household without any real framework for managing money beyond making sure the bills were paid. There was no formal budgeting system at that time. No long-term planning, just constant attention and adjustment. My wife and I were both doing our best, but neither of us had been taught how to build stability, only how to maintain it. We wanted to feel comfortable and we wanted to feel secure, but we didn't have the tools to tell the difference between those two things.

By my mid-twenties, I had two children. They were the greatest blessings in my life, but I wasn't financially prepared for the weight of that responsibility. At a very young age, I found myself with a home, two cars, a growing career, and a salary that still very much read "early career."

Since I'm telling a story about escaping poverty, I should explain how we bought that house. We had virtually no savings at the time. My first wife's parents owned the home, and they'd been renting it out. They sold it to us slightly under market value, then they loaned us the down payment, which we passed along to the bank. The bank then wrote a mortgage for the sale price plus the down payment. We walked away as homeowners with no money down, and my in-laws were made whole when their downpayment loan to us was repaid through the sale. On paper, we owned a home, but in reality, we were leveraging family relationships to create the appearance of stability. The warrior finds a way to make things work. We had no emergency funds, no savings, and no margin, but we had a house.

Despite this, we weren't failing, but we weren't building either. What I recognized later was already true then, that I was operating in the same pattern I had grown up watching. Working harder just to stay in place. The surroundings had changed, but the structure had not, and I didn't question it. This was what responsibility looked like. This was what adulthood required, and if it felt heavy, that only meant I was doing it right.

By the end of my twenties, the pattern was firmly in place. When pressure increased, I looked for ways to advance. When advancement didn't bring relief, I looked for ways to fortify myself against uncertainty. Education, credentials, responsibility; these all felt like tools I could control, so I kept adding them.

I didn't think of this as overextension, I thought of it as preparation. If one layer of stability wasn't enough, I assumed another would be. If the margin didn't appear, then clearly, I haven't earned it yet.

That logic was familiar and it made sense to me. It had always made sense. I wasn't chasing excess, I was chasing safety, but safety never quite arrived.

What I didn't realize then was that I had begun to treat motion itself as protection. Standing still felt irresponsible and slowing down felt dangerous. The idea of not advancing, even briefly, felt like risk, so I didn't pause. I worked more and I learned more. I stacked responsibilities and credentials and experience. I told myself that this was what growth looked like, and for a long time no one questioned it, least of all me.

Chapter 3: Faster Still

Slowing down still felt dangerous.

Poverty in my childhood home existed before I did. I was unaware of its arrival, and I didn't trust that it wouldn't return the same way; quietly, patiently, waiting for a moment of hesitation. In place before I was aware, so I didn't hesitate.

By the time I moved out of bedside nursing, I had already learned how to stack endurance. Long shifts, nights, weekends, and certifications layered on top of responsibility. Skill felt like insulation and knowledge felt like protection.

When my employer began planning a transition to an electronic health record, something in me lit up. I had always been drawn to computers and technology, and I understood the hospital systems and workflows. When the opportunity arose, the organization created a systems engineer role specifically for that transition and offered it to me.

I accepted with the understanding that I would also pursue a computer science degree. I enrolled in the degree program at a local university while already working in the role. The title came first. The degree followed. I was able to take advantage of my employer's tuition reimbursement program to get the degree, but it had annual limits. It took seven years to complete the degree, not because of a lack of ability, but because I couldn't afford to move any faster than that.

A typical week during those seven years included about sixty hours just between work and school. Fifty hours as the systems engineer (I was the only one for a decade) plus another ten for class and coursework. I could only take one class at a time because of the tuition reimbursement limits. Moving faster wasn't financially possible, so I didn't.

I loved the systems engineer work, and I was building a solid career. This wasn't just about escaping something anymore; it was also about building something. The degree was another layer of qualification and another credential that would create more opportunities down the road. It was a very busy role, however. I was on call constantly. Nights, weekends, holidays, and the regular monthly system downtimes that ran from 1:00 a.m. to 3:00 a.m. These were planned maintenance windows that I had to support every month. Sleep during those years was fragmented at best.

During one system upgrade, the installation failed. It was our entire EHR system, and there was significant system performance degradation after bringing the system back up. There was no option to come back to it later. This is a busy hospital environment that operates 24/7. I was awake for about thirty hours straight recovering the system. The next few nights, I only managed three or four hours of sleep each, then it was back to work, back to class, and back to the cycle. It didn't feel heroic, just necessary.

My sleep patterns were always disrupted while working in this role. The monthly maintenance was at least scheduled, so you could plan for it, but being on call 10 out of 14 days in endless cycles meant that I had to be alert for a call anytime, day or night. It was very difficult to sleep knowing I could not truly be unavailable.

At the time, this felt prudent and responsible, another example of making things work inside constraints. What I didn't see was how this further normalized a life built around constant output. Full-time technical work paired with long-term schooling felt familiar by now. I had done this before, and I knew how to endure.

The systems engineer role expanded quickly. We kept adding more and more integrated systems and the complexity increased each time. I became indispensable. Not because I was irreplaceable in theory, but because I was simply the only one in the role. For years, I was *the* systems engineer.

Because of the call schedule, any vacation time had to align with four-day weekends, or I simply stayed on-call while away. By that point in my career, I had never taken a full, uninterrupted week off. Even when my children were born, I returned to work after two weeks. It didn't feel like sacrifice at the time it just felt like responsibility.

Somewhere along the way, my first marriage ended. It didn't end suddenly, and it wasn't a surprise. The mental and emotional processing had started long before the legal separation, so by the time it was official, I was already moving forward. The divorce brought emotional strain and financial disruption, but it didn't slow me down. If anything, it reinforced the need to keep moving. Stability still felt conditional.

I married again a couple years later, before finishing the computer science degree. A new relationship, another home, and eventually, my third child. I was blessed beyond anything I thought possible with my children.

Buying the second house followed a similar pattern. My second wife's parents loaned us the down payment, which they'd be reimbursed for later when the house eventually sold in our divorce. Again, no actual savings. Again, leveraging family support to create the appearance of financial stability. The warrior was resourceful, I'll give him that, but resourcefulness isn't the same as sustainability. I was making things work without building any actual margin. The houses were real, but the stability was borrowed.

Education continued in a surprising way

Life's pace didn't change. After completing the computer science program, I immediately enrolled in an MBA program using my employer's education grant that made the cost almost impossible to ignore. It would only take two years to complete and only cost $5000 out of pocket. I couldn't pass that up. Another credential and another promise of advancement.

The MBA led to something quite unexpected. Immediately after graduating, the program coordinator asked if I would teach a computer science course as an adjunct instructor. I had never imagined myself as a teacher and I only accepted it for the extra money. I really never expected that it would be anything more than this one temporary opportunity.

Within a few short weeks, I was hooked. I absolutely loved this role. What appealed to me was a mix of things. I loved the student engagement, the dialogue, the questions, the moment when something clicked for someone, and I loved the constant learning. Teaching forced me to stay sharp, to keep refining how I explained complex ideas, and to encounter perspectives I hadn't considered. It made me better in a number of ways.

One of the most refreshing things it brought was a space for me to be creative.

Working in technology doesn't foster creativity. Regardless of how creative you may be, you're still working within a coded, confined system. Teaching, on the other hand, not only fosters creativity, but it also encourages it. Creativity bolsters pedagogy, and I loved that.

The computer science class was a good fit considering my previous bachelor's degree and work experience. The very first class session went well, but I also only had my own experience as a student to base that on. I had no frame of reference for how to lead the class or being responsible for the content and lessons, and no training for any of it. Here I was again, just figuring it out on my own. I was way overprepared for that first class and ended up stretching the material I had ready into the next few weeks of classes. Subsequent classes, after realizing that I absolutely loved teaching, were fun and allowed me some moment of escape from the professional life I had been accustomed to. The greatest skill I had at the time, and what I carry through today, is being able to take apart a complex concept and help students learn it in manageable pieces and then put it all back together with understanding. I tend to be a storyteller teacher, so much of my teaching is also done through personal experience, application, and tie-ins to the "real world".

But the most impactful part was knowing I was significantly affecting the students' lives in a positive way. That mattered to me in a way the technical work never had. I was giving the students tools and knowledge they would build on to change their lives, some of them possibly in ways my own life was changed by education. It was a different kind of connection, and I thrived in the role

Teaching felt different. It was energizing and meaningful, and I was good at it. I began taking on more classes, and then more schools. Over the next several years I went on to teach adjunct courses for seven different schools, all while still working full time in my regular role. Not all seven schools at once, of course. At most, I taught for three schools at the same time, but I was teaching at a full-time load and didn't know it. No one ever explained what "full-time" meant in higher education. I simply kept saying yes.

I didn't have a limit in mind when I started saying yes to more classes, I just kept accepting opportunities until I found the limit physically. One year I taught fourteen classes. Most of the classes I taught were eight weeks in length, with a few full-term courses mixed in. The load was staggering, but I managed it. That was a skillset I had been building my entire life.

This is the time in my career when I would work all day as a systems engineer, then 3 evenings each week after work I would drive to campuses that were an hour or more away. These were 8-week classes, so that ended up being 6 spring classes, 2 summer classes, and then 6 fall classes. There was no structure to my time that I created, I simply went where I was required to be at any given time. My schedule was not under my control during those years.

Life's dynamics keep changing

A few years after finishing the MBA program, my second marriage ended. By then, I was deep into the teaching acceleration, stacking classes and institutions on top of my full-time systems work. Another emotional rupture, another financial hit, and again, I responded the only way I knew how, by carrying more.

It was more automatic than conscious. We were together for a much shorter time than my first marriage. There were a lot of details to work out, but I was not deterred from the work. There was little processing time, just immediate forward motion. The process was familiar.

A few years later, I got married for the third time. It felt entirely different. Not in the sense of "this time will be different" as a hopeful wish, but in the sense that it already was different in every aspect. I had known my wife for most of my life, longer than I had known my first wife. We had a ton in common, deeply held mutual beliefs, and a shared understanding of what mattered.

We talked at a much deeper level. There were no games, nothing hidden, no agendas, and we agreed on major things like family, money, religion/spirituality. We liked the same types of entertainment and enjoyed spending time in similar ways. Ironically, she was also adopted into her own family as a baby, so we had this rather unique thing in common. She had two kids of her own that were close in age to my two older kids, that I would quickly love as if they were my own.

This wasn't another attempt at the same pattern. This was something else.

Around that period, I was promoted to a Team Lead position and hired a second systems engineer. The pattern repeated itself exactly as before. More responsibility, more income, more pressure, and more people depending on me. A few years later I was promoted again, this time to manager of my department. This was the highest income I had ever earned. The most authority I had ever held. The most responsibility I had ever carried, and I was good at it.

I learned to optimize under heavy load, to manage complexity, and to hold systems together through vigilance rather than design. The organization adjusted around my presence, and I adjusted around its demands in return. At the time, it felt like respect, like value. I was treated very well by that employer, and I had incredible opportunities during my career there. The indispensability felt like validation, not entrapment.

During this period, as well as through the CS degree, the MBA, the teaching explosion, the marriages, and the promotions, somehow it all felt manageable. Strained certainly, but manageable. The more I did, the more I felt like I could do. At times, it felt like a challenge, like a test to see how much I could juggle simultaneously. A terrible test of endurance and capacity, but one I kept taking anyway.

No one told me to slow down. Not because they didn't care, but because I never let anyone see the full picture. From the outside, it probably looked like I was busy but not overwhelmed. I was genuinely happy, despite the increasing pressure and pace.

That's the insidious part. I was happy. The work was meaningful and the advancements were real. The competence I had built was undeniable, but happiness and sustainability are not the same thing, and I wouldn't understand that until much later.

From the outside, it looked like success. From the inside, it felt like acceleration without brakes.

There was no dramatic collapse. No obvious warning light. Just the quiet tightening of a life built entirely around motion. Faster still felt like the only safe option.

Chapter 4: When More Still Isn't Enough

Feeling competent in the chaos

By the time I moved into leadership, the pattern was no longer subtle. The pay raises came with relief at first, but it also came with more responsibility, more people to support, bigger systems to oversee, and more outcomes to own. I was moving everything forward, but still not creating any margin in my life.

For once, however, there was no imposter syndrome; no sense that I had stumbled into something I wasn't ready for. I had pursued the MBA specifically to prepare for leadership, and I had made that intention known years earlier, so when the opportunity came, I was first in line, and I felt like I had earned it.

That validation mattered. It confirmed that the path I had chosen with the degrees, the certifications, the years of stacking credentials and competence had worked. I had proven myself. The effort had translated into something tangible. For a brief moment, it felt like arrival.

But by the second or third year of management, something had shifted. Life wasn't changing the way I had expected. The income was higher and the title was more prestigious, but the responsibility was also greater. The relief I had been waiting for, the sense that "someday" had finally come, never materialized.

I was still managing. Still vigilant. Still holding systems together through attention rather than margin. The salary hadn't changed how safe I felt, it had only raised the floor on what I was now required to maintain. The same cycle was playing out. Work harder, take on more, earn more, and carry more.

Tragedy and acceleration

Around this time, our son, my stepson, died by suicide. It was catastrophic. There isn't a version of that sentence that isn't heavy, and there isn't a way to move past it cleanly. The loss changed everything, even as the world around us continued to move on.

In the aftermath, my wife stopped working for a while. Grief does not respect schedules or budgets. She needed time to process a loss that no parent should have to carry, and there was no timeline for when she'd be ready to return. I supported that completely. It was the right decision, and it wasn't up for discussion.

But the practical reality didn't pause while we grieved. Our household income dropped by roughly 40% at the exact moment emotional and practical demands were at their highest. The bills didn't stop. The extra teaching income helped, but it wasn't enough to fully bridge the gap.

I had to take on more classes. Not because I wanted to, but because the math required it. Every adjunct course I could force into the schedule became necessary rather than optional. The heavy load I was already carrying got heavier, but there was no other choice. Someone had to keep the systems running.

The household still needed to function. Meals needed to happen, kids needed rides, attention, and normalcy wherever and however normalcy was possible. Work still expected results and my team didn't know how the burden had changed at home, and I didn't tell them. I showed up every day as if nothing was any different, because that's what the role demanded.

At home I became the anchor point for everything practical. Not because my wife wasn't capable, but because she was dealing with something that required all her energy just to survive. I handled what I could handle, and I made decisions that needed making. I kept motion going because stopping at this point was not possible.

This was when the pattern really solidified. The belief that I couldn't stop, that everything depended on me continuing exactly as I was. If I slowed down, if I admitted I was stretched too thin, the whole structure might collapse. So, I didn't slow down. I found capacity I didn't know I had, or more accurately, I borrowed against capacity I didn't actually have.

At the same time, over those blurred years, the shape of our family was changing. My oldest daughter moved to Alaska with her fiancé where he was stationed in the Army. My stepdaughter graduated from college and moved to Florida. My son moved out but stayed nearby, eventually entering the corrections officer academy, with its own intensity and risk. Not long after, all three were married and beginning families of their own. Our family wasn't just dispersing; it was expanding remotely.

From the outside, it might have looked like pressure was easing. There were fewer people in the house, and our older children were launching into adulthood. Inside, it felt like fragmentation and the distance brought new expenses. Travel. Logistics. Worry.

Parental support didn't end when children moved out or married, it just changed form.

Alaska, Florida, different time zones, different lives, different crises we couldn't respond to in person. Plane tickets when someone needed us there. Hotels, rental cars, and the financial cost of distance added up, but that wasn't the heavy part.

The heavy part was the emotional distance that came with geographical separation. Phone calls replaced conversations around the table. There were updates instead of daily presence. We were happy for them and proud of their independence, their marriages, their own families starting, but the house that had once been too full was now too quiet, and that quiet made everything else louder.

The grief, the financial pressure, and the awareness that we were now in a different phase of life; one where we couldn't gather everyone together without significant planning and expense. The family hadn't ended, but it had fundamentally changed shape.

And in the middle of all that change, I was still the one expected to keep everything stable. I was still managing my team at work, still teaching multiple classes, and still making sure the bills were paid and the budget balanced and that there was nothing

visible broken. The fragmentation wasn't
just geographical, it was internal. I was
holding pieces together that didn't fit the
same way anymore.

Reassembled

A few years following this, my wife was back
to full-time work, and our household
income reached the highest it had ever been,
but our debt had grown considerably during
the years leading up. Between my
management salary, the extra courses I was
teaching, and my wife's salary, the numbers
finally looked like something people
associate with success. Not abundance,
exactly, but strength and added capacity. It
felt like we had the ability to handle things,
and in a narrow sense, that was true.

We didn't miss any payments and the bills
were paid on time. Emergencies didn't
immediately spiral into crisis. The pressure
that had once been loud was now quieter,
more contained. Debt no longer felt urgent.
It felt permanent, like something to manage,
not escape. Strangely, it felt comfortable.
This is a danger zone.

At our peak, our household income was
approaching $200,000 a year. On paper,
that should have changed everything, but at
the same time, our monthly debt payments,
which were entirely from credit cards and a

401(k) loan, were about $3,200. That wasn't a temporary spike, it was a fixed obligation and one we had learned to live with.

When debt becomes a fixed line item instead of an emergency, it stops demanding change. It simply demands maintenance. I never stopped tracking the debt. If anything, I was more engaged with the budget than ever and I knew exactly where we stood every month. I monitored every dollar, every payment, and every balance. The problem wasn't awareness; it was that the debt wasn't moving. We were paying it reliably and consistently, but it wasn't shrinking at the rate I had once believed it would. It became a permanent feature of the financial landscape. Something to manage indefinitely rather than escape.

I had become excellent at budgeting. Not the kind that builds wealth, but the kind that keeps complex systems running. Multiple incomes and household expenses that shifted with distance and circumstances. I could make it all work on paper.

The budget spreadsheet was a work of art. All the income streams tracked to the penny. Every expense categorized. Every payment scheduled. Uneven teaching income smoothed across months. My wife's overtime factored in when available. It all balanced and every month, the numbers worked.

What didn't show up in the spreadsheet was the stress of making it work. The mental load of knowing that one missed paycheck, one big unexpected expense, one deviation from the plan could cascade into crisis.

I was exceptional at making complex systems function. That's what I did at work, and that's what I did at home, but there's a difference between a system that functions and a system that's healthy. Mine functioned, but it wasn't healthy. It required constant attention, constant vigilance, constant course correction.

Smoke and mirrors

The $200,000 income should have meant security. Instead, it meant that I had successfully built a life that required $200,000 simply to function. The margin that should have come with higher income never materialized because the obligations had been scaled right alongside it.

Without debt, even a considerably lower income can feel exceptional because margin isn't just financial, it's also temporal, emotional, and relational. It gives you the freedom to make choices based on what matters rather than just what's required.

That's not a trade-off most people recognize until they've experienced both sides.

It's not just about the budget. It's also about time, relationships, health, and decision-making. Every dimension of life is impacted by margin. High income with debt means you're locked into maintaining that income. You can't slow down, you can't take risks, you can't pivot. The debt demands feeding, and that feeding requires the income stream to continue exactly as it is.

Here's what I didn't understand then and what most people don't understand about the relationship between income and debt; that debt has such a massive impact on margin that even at your highest income, you can experience the least amount of freedom. The $200,000 we were earning gave us less actual margin, less flexibility, fewer options, and less peace than I would later have while earning less, but without debt.

Ironically it was during this same period that I started teaching budgeting to others. The cognitive dissonance was real, but I rationalized it easily enough. My situation was different, more complex. My income was higher, but so were my obligations. The principles I was teaching were sound; they just hadn't worked for me yet because I was in a unique position. After all, a doctor with cancer can still treat cancer patients. That is how I rationalized it anyway.

People started asking me for financial advice. Colleagues, friends, people who had heard I was good with budgeting and investing. They had no idea I was carrying significant debt myself. What started as informal conversations eventually became something more intentional. I started a small financial advising practice, though calling it a "practice" feels too formal for what it was.

I never marketed it. There was no advertising or growth strategy. It grew purely through word of mouth, and I kept it that way on purpose. Small, manageable, and intentional. I was teaching finance and economics classes then, gaining knowledge both academically and through my own messy lived experience.

The work felt meaningful and the principles I shared were sound. The strategies worked, and I believed in them. I just couldn't seem to apply them to my own situation with the same clarity I brought to others. The gap was real, but I had rationalized it.

I told students to avoid debt at all costs, and I meant it. I believed it then, and I still do now. My own children were my first students in this regard. The advice I gave was based on sound personal finance principles, but not on my own experience, so there was a gap between what I taught and what I practiced. I saw the gap, I just didn't know how to close it yet.

Income illusion

Our life required this persistent level of income to continue. It required the extra teaching load to remain heavy. It required endurance, not as a temporary measure, but as a permanent state. The sprint had become a marathon, and because I had proven I could do it, the system quietly organized itself around that assumption.

This is where the illusion takes hold. Not the illusion of luxury, but the illusion of security. The belief was that because things are functioning, they are stable. That because you're earning well, you're safe. That because you're managing the load, the load is manageable. But there was still no real margin.

The realization that this wasn't sustainable didn't arrive all at once. It came slowly, like fog lifting in the morning. Gradual enough that I could keep moving while it cleared. There was no dramatic moment where I thought this has to stop, just a quiet accumulation of signals. The irritability. The health problems. The sense that every decision felt heavier than it should. The awareness that I was holding everything together through sheer vigilance, and that vigilance was no longer enough.

The system had quietly organized itself around the assumption that I could keep performing, and I reinforced that assumption every day by making it look manageable. I never wanted the struggle to show. Not at work, and especially not at home. If I let people see how thin the margin really was, they might question whether I could carry the load, so I kept it hidden. Not dishonestly, just privately. No one questioned my capacity because I gave them no reason to, and at the time, I didn't question this either. I couldn't afford to. Everything I had built now depended on me continuing exactly as I was, so I did, and for a while, it worked.

The raises and promotions mattered. On paper, the trajectory was undeniable. I was making more money than I ever had, and by a measure that would have once felt unimaginable. But what didn't change was how safe I felt.

Each increase in income came paired with an increase in obligation. The numbers grew, but so did the surface area of risk. I didn't feel reckless with money. I was careful, methodical, and I tracked everything, but none of that produced relief.

It produced vigilance, and vigilance is not the same thing as security.

Looking back, this is where the illusion further took hold. I assumed that earning more would eventually flip some internal switch from anxious to settled, from alert to at ease. It never did because nothing about my relationship with money had actually changed. I had just raised the stakes. By then, I had become very good at maintenance. Bills were always paid. Crises were avoided. Schedules were held together, even if barely so. The household functioned, and from the outside, it looked like stability. Inside, however, it felt like a balance that required constant correction.

When simply keeping everything upright becomes the goal, you stop asking whether the structure itself makes sense. You confuse motion with progress. You start to believe that if nothing is falling apart, you must be doing well, even while nothing is being built. This is the first danger zone, and it's the hardest one to recognize.

It isn't collapse, it's functionality without margin. It's high income paired with high fixed obligations. It's being able to make everything work as long as nothing unexpected happens. It had become a perpetual cycle where the status quo now required the status quo to continue.

On a daily basis, it feels like holding your breath between paychecks, between decisions, between the next thing that might break. It feels like avoiding conversations about savings and retirement because those topics aren't realistic and talking about them just adds to the stress.

Debt illusion

Debt had become normal by then. Not urgent, not panic, just present. Another line item to manage. Another fixed cost to plan around. I wasn't running from it anymore; I was living with it. That normalization is what makes this phase so deceptive. Nothing is on fire, but everything is flammable.

My wife saw it. She was extraordinarily supportive of what I said needed to be done, but she also checked in frequently, making sure I was truly well, not just maintaining the appearance of wellness. Sometimes I wasn't well, and she could see that. Other times I was able to hide it, or at least I thought so.

During this period, my life didn't reflect a household income that gave us comfort. It didn't appear as a life of abundance. There were no visible markers of high income. We still drove used cars, wore aging clothing, ate common food. Nothing about our lifestyle suggested we were approaching $200,000 a year in household income.

We looked stable, maybe even frugal, but what wasn't visible was the strain underneath it all. The monthly debt payments that quietly consumed what should have been margin. The constant vigilance required to keep everything functioning. The way every unexpected expense triggered stress even though, on paper, we should have been able to absorb it easily. I wouldn't understand until much later that this wasn't the only danger zone. It was just the first.

Chapter 5: The Limits Appear

Stacking and compounding

For a long time, nothing actually broke. That's what made this phase so difficult to recognize. There was no single failure, no dramatic collapse, no moment when everything fell apart and demanded immediate attention. Life kept functioning. Work continued. Bills got paid.

Responsibilities were met, but something had changed.

By this point, our household had reached its highest level of complexity. We had five kids, four of them driving at the same time, which meant six cars in our driveway at any given time, including mine and my wife's. We all drove used cars that were well-used, and we had managed to pay cash for all of them. That felt like a source of pride, but the reality was simpler, there was no way to force another payment into the budget.

Not having car loans didn't make owning them free, however. Insurance with four young drivers was staggering. They were all considered high-risk simply because of their age. Then there were maintenance and repairs such as brake pads, batteries, tires, oil changes, and check engine lights. I did most of the work myself, but not because I enjoyed it. I had the skills to do most of it and a mechanic would cost what we couldn't afford to pay. Oil changes in the driveway and brake jobs on jack stands. Replacing alternators and starters in the winter when batteries died.

There were times when I'd come home from work and spend the evening under one of the cars, fixing whatever had failed that day so it could get someone to school or work the next morning. Six cars, all well-used, all requiring attention that I had to provide myself.

Coordinating four teenagers with vehicles was its own job, but there was also the constant calculation of who needed the driveway clear and when, whose schedule took priority.

Other expenses multiplied quietly as well. Groceries, health insurance, doctor visits, dental work, glasses, braces, prescriptions, clothes, school fees, sports and activity costs, modest plans for college or vocational training. Even the basics, like laundry detergent, dish soap, cleaning supplies, every normal household cost amplified by volume. There was no extravagance here, just volume.

None of this is meant to place responsibility on the kids. They weren't the problem. They were living normal lives in a household that was stretched thin. The strain came from the structure around them, not from them.

When my wife and I married, the house had three bedrooms and two bathrooms. To make space for a blended family of seven, we finished the entire basement, adding an additional three bedrooms, a bathroom, a second laundry area, open space, and storage with fully finished walls and ceilings, and tile flooring. The work was done mostly by me and one other person, paid for with an equity loan and a growing stack of credit card charges.

The renovation took about a year, but we started before fully integrating the households, before we really understood what we were signing up for. The work had to happen while life continued around it. Nothing was put on hold just because we were tearing apart the basement.

I remember at the beginning of the project when the lumber and the drywall were delivered. After we got it all loaded into the basement, I just stood looking at it thinking "how am I going to do all of this?" Hiring a construction crew was not an option. We had one hired worker and me to do it all. Fortunately, I worked on my dad's construction crew for a short time early in my college career (before the ortho tech job), so I had enough skills for framing, drywall, simple wiring, etc. The ability to get all that done, somehow forced into my already impossible schedule seemed like a monumental task, but somehow, we did it.

The work happened in fragments. I'd get home from work around 5:00, change clothes, and head downstairs. Most nights I could get two or three hours in before exhaustion forced me to stop. Weekends were often eight-hour days in the basement, breaking only when my back demanded it or when family obligations couldn't be postponed.

My hands stayed permanently scraped and callused. My lower back ached constantly from the lifting, the bending, the awkward positions required to work in tight spaces. I'd wake up stiff most mornings, stretch it out, and keep going. The work wasn't elegant, but it was functional, and that's all it needed to be.

The hired worker that had been helping me was reliable, but he had his own schedule and his own constraints. This was side work for him too, so when he couldn't be there, I worked alone. None of this was happening in isolation. I was still managing my full-time job, still teaching adjunct classes when

I could fit them in, still trying to be present for a family that was adjusting to living together. The renovation wasn't a project, it was a second job that came with no paycheck, only debt.

The entire time, I kept asking myself the same question. How am I going to get all this done?

There was no margin for error. No budget for professionals. No time to pause and regroup. We worked in fragments of time that didn't exist, using money we didn't have. Every material purchase went on a credit card. Every delay meant more time living in construction chaos with dust everywhere, tools scattered, the basement unusable while we worked.

Every day required extra effort in ways that weren't always visible but were always felt. The equity loan and credit card financing felt like a necessary evil. There was no other way. The family needed a place to function, and this was how we made it happen.

It didn't trigger alarm bells, at least not the kind that made me stop. It triggered the kind that I learned to ignore. This wasn't a renovation for comfort or style, it was an attempt to keep the household functioning.

My employer knew very little about what I was carrying. I'm a private person in that regard. I never let them see how thinly I was stretched. I didn't frame it as strength or stoicism; it was just how I operated. Keep the systems running and don't let the personal bleed into the professional.

That boundary worked until it didn't.

Signals

Around this time, my body began pushing back. I was diagnosed with a fatty liver that was entirely dietary in origin. Long days, constant movement, travel to teach, and convenience foods grabbed between obligations. Healthy routines never stood a chance with my schedule. I was always moving, always tired, always choosing what was fast over what was good.

The fatty liver diagnosis came from something I noticed myself. I was taking a shower and just happened to notice it when looking down. My abdomen looked unbalanced. Not dramatically, but enough that I could see it. I initially just called my doctor's office. They recommended I get seen in the ER and have a CT done to be sure it wasn't anything serious. Thankfully, it was just an enlarged, fatty liver at the upper end of the normal measurement. That's not to dismiss it. This was a clear early sign that my lifestyle was affecting my health. In this case, it was my diet and how I fit eating into my schedule instead of prioritizing my health. I worked in healthcare too long to dismiss abdominal swelling and knew that putting anything off with your health is just inviting trouble. Between healthcare, construction, and technology, I gained a ton of experience that would help me in many parts of my daily life.

I made changes in my diet and my routine. Small changes, and I managed them, but even that felt like another thing to monitor, another system to maintain. Another consequence of a life built around motion instead of recovery.

The disc rupture was different.

I had been having sharp pains in my lower back for a while, the kind you stretch through, the kind you tell yourself will go away if you're just careful. Years of physical labor around the house, car repairs. yard work, lifting and carrying because paying someone else felt irresponsible had taken its toll.

One morning, I woke up and couldn't stand up straight. The pain was immediate and total. I tried to roll to the edge of the bed to get my feet on the floor, and my back seized completely. I couldn't straighten myself enough to walk. I called out to my wife, and she woke and saw me hunched over, unable to move more than a few inches without the pain stopping me cold.

"I need to go to the ER," I told her. "Something's wrong."

The drive to the ER was excruciating. Every bump in the road sent a shock through my spine. I couldn't sit upright. I leaned forward in the passenger seat, bracing myself against the dashboard, trying to find any position that didn't make it worse. There wasn't one. The pain was like a hot knife lodged in my lower back, twisting with every movement.

When we got to the ER, I called in some favors. I'd worked with most of the staff when I was in healthcare, and I knew the ER doctor on shift that morning. I even knew the spine surgeon who was on call. They moved quickly. The MRI showed what I already suspected but didn't want to confirm, the L4-L5 disc had fully ruptured. An emergency discectomy surgery was underway.

The surgery went well. I awoke with zero pain, which felt miraculous. It also occurred to me in a humorous way how much I enjoyed the anesthesia sleep! I never slept that well on my own. For a brief while I felt rested and pain-free.

The surgeon was direct afterward, no lifting, take time off, and let your body recover. I was sent home with lifting restrictions and instructions to rest for at least six weeks before considering any physical work.

Soon after surgery, the basement flooded due to a bad storm that knocked out our power, and thus, the sump pump stopped working. There was a water-siphon backup, but it couldn't keep up with the incoming flow of water. My older daughter and granddaughter were staying with us at the time because her husband was deployed overseas. She noticed the flooding when her dog jumped down off the bed in the middle of the night and she heard the splash. She called me on the phone, and I could hear the urgency in her voice. This wasn't something that could wait, and there was no one else to handle it.

I went downstairs to find about 6 inches of water in our fully finished basement. I wasn't supposed to be lifting anything over ten pounds, but I spent the next several hours moving water. Every movement pulled at the fresh surgical site, and I knew I was violating the restrictions. I did it anyway because, as I had become accustomed to doing, I prioritized what felt like an urgent need over my own health.

The surgeon had also told me to lose weight because having extra weight on the spine wasn't helping. I lost about fifty pounds over the next year, but I didn't restrict myself physically much beyond that initial week. I was back to teaching within a few days. Back to managing my team. Back to working on the house whenever something needed attention.

The lesson didn't land the way they should have. My body had sent a clear signal that I had reached a limit, and I had heard it, I just chose to keep moving anyway.

Besides these more acute events, sleep was poor, headaches were frequent, and irritability crept in often and sometimes suddenly. One moment still stands out to me. My son called to tell me he had slid on ice while driving and been in a minor accident. He was safe and no one was hurt, but I exploded. Not because of the accident, but because everything inside me was already stretched too thin. I gave him a reaction he didn't deserve, and in return, he gave me grace that I didn't deserve, and he didn't make me work for it. That stuck with me.

I knew right away I had gone overboard. I saw it for what it was, which was not anger at him, but anger at the weight of everything else I was carrying at the time. He just happened to be the person who called at the very moment I couldn't hold it anymore. What struck me most was how he responded. He was calm and stoic, almost like he understood that whatever I was going through at that moment had nothing to do with him.

We didn't talk about it immediately after, but at some point later, I apologized. We didn't try to unpack it. He's a very smart kid and we have a quiet, but deep bond. I like to say he let me off with a warning, ha! But going forward, I was more aware of my own tipping point.

Still, it didn't change how I operated. I felt the shame then, but I kept pushing. The moment became another thing I carried instead of a signal to stop. This wasn't burnout in the way people usually describe it. It wasn't about hating my work or wanting to quit. It was something quieter and more dangerous. I had reached the limits of capacity. I was still disciplined, still organized, still "holding it together", but the capacity was gone. Every unexpected expense triggered stress. Every deviation required adjustment. Every new responsibility felt heavier than the last.

You cannot spreadsheet your way out of a nervous system shaped by scarcity and hypervigilance.

The strategies that had kept me moving forward for decades were no longer working. Not because they were wrong, but because they were being asked to do more than they were designed to do. Endurance had carried me far, but endurance is not infinite. For the first time, I began to sense that something would have to change, not because I wanted it to, but because it simply could no longer stay the same.

My wife and I talked about it sometimes. Not in crisis language, and not with urgency, just quiet conversations about how things needed to change eventually. Someday. When the debt eased. When the kids were fully launched. When the pressure lets up. We never labeled it as unsustainable because if we called it that, if we said it out loud, then we'd have to do something about it, and I didn't know what that something could possibly be. I only knew how to keep going.

So, I kept looking forward to "someday". Someday the load will lighten. Someday the income will catch up. Someday I'd feel like I had margin instead of just managing systems on the edge of capacity. The belief that someday would arrive on its own kept me moving longer than it should have.

Interlude: When Endurance Stops Working

If you've made it this far there's a good chance something in you recognizes what's being described. Not the details or the specific career or numbers or circumstances, but in the pattern.

There's a moment, quiet and often unnoticed when effort stops producing relief. When discipline still works mechanically but is no longer liberating. When doing more doesn't feel noble, it just feels heavy. Unfortunately, this is usually the point where people double down. They optimize harder, tighten routines, and add systems. They push through because pushing through has always been the answer. Endurance has worked before, so why wouldn't it work now? And that is exactly what I did.

Doubling down reinforces that the current behavior is effective without having to acknowledge that it may not be. This is a classic pattern known as escalation of commitment. You see it anytime failure is imminent, but so much time, energy, money, and emotion have been invested that you continue on the same path all the way through to collapse.

Think of someone who has had a car for a while that they really like and have spent a lot of time and money keeping it running, but it's requiring more frequent repairs, with increasing cost. How long do you stay with it before deciding to stop? The sunk costs, both emotional and financial, make it difficult to walk away, even when continuing becomes more expensive than moving on. We see this even more pronounced in relationship that are past failure. How often have you seen someone stay in a relationship because of the investments of time, energy, and emotion, even if it's obviously not working?

I doubled down every time I took on another class to teach, even when I already felt spread too thin. I doubled down every time I used a credit card with the delusion that this was a unique situation, that I'd just pay for it later and never do it again. I also doubled down on opportunities that would improve my skills and education. I doubled down on the idea that no matter what the elevation of the treadmill, I could run fast enough to stay on it. I had put too much into this life to slow down.

What would it have taken for me to stop before circumstances forced it? That's a good question, because I had no intention of stopping. I hadn't considered what a hard stop would even look like on that path. Probably a heart attack or a stroke, or an ultimatum from my family. Something catastrophic enough to make continued motion impossible.

My wife was always very supportive and sensitive to times when I needed a break or just some downtime for myself. She never came close to giving an ultimatum, at least not that I'm aware of. But the absence of external pressure to stop only meant I had to generate that pressure internally, something I proved incapable of or unwilling to do at the time.

That's the danger of doubling down. You remove the possibility of choosing to stop before something forces you to. Because endurance has limits, and not the kind you can train past.

Endurance is excellent at surviving short-term threats, but it is terrible at sustaining a life without margin. Let me clarify the distinction, because many people think endurance and capacity are the same thing.

Endurance is your ability to function at a certain level and on a certain path with the resources you have. Capacity is the limit of those resources. With endless capacity, endurance would be theoretically infinite.

But we all have capacity restrictions that endurance can't overcome. I tested those limits, believing I could stretch capacity through sheer willpower. That's when I learned that no amount of mental, physical, financial, or behavioral endurance can overcome capacity.

Think of it like a sprinter versus a distance runner. The sprinter relies more on intense, short-term capacity, expending all of their energy once, while a distance runner expends their energy over a longer distance, but at a more controlled pace. In my case, I had a good deal of both, but capacity tends to limit us before endurance does when you're constantly accelerating. You can't sprint for a marathon distance, and that's what I was trying to do.

Real safety is found in increasing capacity while using endurance strategically to support it. That's how margin is created. Endurance feels empowering, but it's an unsustainable feedback loop without capacity. The more you manage, the more it feels like you can manage until you can't. I didn't find that line until I stepped over it.

Having excess capacity, having margin, sometimes feels inefficient at first. Resources that exist simply to provide comfort and peace don't make sense to the warrior. Why have savings sitting idle when you could be using them? Why would you turn down opportunities when you have the skills to take advantage? Why rest when there's work to be done?

Once the importance of margin is realized, it feels necessary and becomes a priority. I could argue that acceleration paired with endurance worked to free me from the poverty I was desperate to escape, but I accelerated far longer than I needed to, and I didn't slow down until I had no ability to continue.

More capacity was badly needed during the time my wife had to stop working after our son's death. If I had the capacity with time, or just my physical ability to handle more extra work during this time, it would have eased our financial strain while my wife wasn't working. It simply wasn't there. I could not do one more thing beyond what I was already doing. Extra capacity would have eased our lives significantly during that period, but it had all been consumed in the service of endurance.

If your nervous system learned early that stability was fragile, that every problem had to be immediately managed or they would certainly become emergencies, and that rest was something you earned only after everything else was done, then motion and endurance likely became your default settings. You learned to stay alert, to anticipate, and to compensate. It probably also made you competent, reliable, and capable. It may have even made you successful.

But endurance cannot be a substitute for capacity. Capacity supports margin, while endurance with acceleration consumes it. And when margin disappears, everything becomes louder. Decisions, emotions, responsibilities, even silence. This is why exhaustion often feels moralized. It's why people say they're tired but still functioning. It's why collapse doesn't look dramatic, it looks like irritability, health problems, impatience with small disruptions, or a sense that life has become unmanageably narrow.

This is not weakness, it's physics. A system without slack cannot absorb shock. If something in this story feels uncomfortably familiar, this interlude is not asking you to change anything yet. It's asking you simply to take notice of how much your life is organized around vigilance instead of intention.

What should you look for? Do you seem preoccupied with monitoring? That could include your budget if you use one, or your bank app, checking your balance several times a day. Do you feel uneasy letting

anything sit for more than a couple of days,
like the mail or receipts? Are you utilizing
autopay, or do you feel the need to control
payment dates to ensure the money will be
there? Do you have any automation built
into your life, or are you focused on
controlling everything you can because you
feel you need to? Do you stretch everything
in your life to the limit, like time, money,
and work?

These aren't signs of competence. They're
signs of vigilance. Other signs may show up
as physical feedback, like elevated anxiety,
high blood pressure, and metabolic issues.
These are all indicators that you've
organized your life around vigilance. You
don't have time to take care of yourself
properly, or at least you haven't prioritized
your time in order to do so.

What about behavioral patterns? Appearing
distracted or unfocused because you're
constantly running through it all in your
head. The inability to be fully present
because part of you is always monitoring,
calculating, preparing for the next thing that
might go wrong. You're always thinking two
steps ahead of what's in front of you right
now.

Not being able to enjoy time away because
in the back of your mind you're still focused
on the micro-details you needed to get away

from in the first place. I used to take my laptop with me any time we went somewhere overnight, even if it was just for one night, because I felt like I had to be able to react to anything immediately. There was no true "away" for me.

What I noticed first when I finally had space to see these patterns was that despite feeling well-organized, in reality I was not very organized at all. I was micromanaging my entire life, and that isn't organization, it's hypervigilance. True organization allows you to automate, to rest, and to trust what you've put in place. Notice how often "if I can just get through this" has become a long-term strategy. Notice whether rest still feels dangerous, or undeserved, or inefficient. Notice whether your definition of strength leaves any room for you.

I know what you might be thinking, "But I have to keep going. I have no choice." I completely understand that feeling. I lived in it for over thirty years. The reality is that at this very moment, that may be true. But at some point, you have to look up and see where you're headed and decide if your current behavior is taking you where you want to go or just reinforcing that you have to keep going for the sake of motion.

You may not be able to afford to stop today, but you can decide today to stop enabling behaviors that perpetuate the cycle. You can outline a clear vision for what a peaceful life looks like and identify the changes, no matter how minor, you could make today that support that new path.

Can you at least create a quiet space with a little time set aside to focus only on this for a moment? I'll help you...you can.

Some things are simply out of your control, like medical costs, employment gaps, and circumstances that truly limit your options. For those scenarios, I would suggest taking advantage of any family, community and social support available to you. Those situations are difficult and real. But for others, the smallest changes can start the process.

The biggest question to answer about not being able to afford to stop is, stop what? What are you moving toward or away from? Where are you today in relation to that destination? That orientation can be the start of it all.

I was running away from something, and I had passed the point of being away from it long before I stopped to measure the distance. By then, I was running on habits and behaviors reinforced in the process. Habits and behaviors that were helpful in the very beginning but no longer warranted.

The threat was gone, but the response conditioning remained.

The shift that follows, away from constant motion and toward something more deliberate, doesn't begin with action. It begins with recognition, and recognition quietly allows what becomes possible next. Change often starts with recognition of a problem when you have the insight to analyze it. This book is designed to help you proactively recognize what no longer works so you can work toward the changes you need.

What becomes possible is developing healthier behaviors that truly support you rather than undermine you. Does recognition alone change anything? I think recognition changes your alignment. That may not appear outwardly as anything different, but behavioral changes start on the inside long before they're noticed on the outside.

How long does it take? For me, it took several months for my posture to change after I identified how I was operating. These are deep-seated neural connections and patterns that have to undergo deliberate revision before those changes are felt. Recognition doesn't solve the problem immediately, but it makes solving the problem possible, and sometimes, that's exactly what you need.

Chapter 6: Unwinding

By the time everything began to feel unsustainable, nothing on the surface looked broken. My wife was back to full-time work, and our income was high again. The highest income we've ever had, in fact. I was still managing my department, while teaching heavily on the side. But the numbers were deceiving and the process to continue supporting it all was unsustainable in ways that could not be ignored.

What did that unsustainability actually look like? It looked like constant motion with little rest. It looked like every action and reaction for the purpose of maintenance, not rest or recovery. It looked like life was all gas and no brake.

Here's what a typical day looked like at peak warrior. Not the worst day, just a normal Tuesday.

Morning (5:00 AM - 7:00 AM)

I'd wake up before the alarm most days, usually around 4:30 AM or so. Not because I was rested, but because my mind was already running through the day. First thought, check email on my phone as soon as I'm out of bed. Second thought, open the banking app, check the balance to make sure nothing unexpectedly hit overnight.

Shower while mentally rehearsing meetings, conversations, and problems to solve. Breakfast was just a coffee or fast food in the car because there wasn't time to eat at home. The commute meant phone calls with direct reports, reviewing my calendar for the day at red lights, mentally preparing for the first meeting. I was already exhausted before arriving at work.

Workday (7:30 AM - 4:00 PM)

Back-to-back meetings with little transition time between them, and no lunch break. I'd typically eat at my desk while responding to emails. Meetings were time to multitask just to get things done, even though we've learned that multitasking is not truly efficient, but it was necessary. Conversations were often interrupted by the next urgency. I was never truly ahead, always catching up and just slightly behind. The feeling wasn't productivity; it was nearly drowning while appearing functional, but I wouldn't let anyone see that side of it. Like the 80's Gillette commercial said, "Never let them see you sweat."

Evening (5:00 PM - 9:30 PM)

Home by 10:30 p.m. after teaching, if I was lucky, or home by 5:00 p.m. if I didn't have class. My family would ask about my day, but my mind was still at work, still running through what didn't get finished, what was waiting for me tomorrow. I'd check email "just once", which turned into thirty minutes or more. Then I'd prep for the next class after dinner. Grade papers while half-watching TV with my wife, physically present but mentally elsewhere. Another budget check before bed, because I had always checked it before bed. I'd lay there mentally reviewing tomorrow's schedule, replaying today's conversations, and planning solutions to problems that might not even exist. Sleep came around 11:00 PM if I was lucky, and the quality was poor.

Weekend (Barely Different)

Saturday meant catching up on work I couldn't finish during the week, working on the basement or other home projects, prepping for next week's classes, updating the budget, reviewing spending, and planning the month ahead. All of this in addition to the "normal" things like grocery shopping, laundry, any cleaning that could be done, car repairs, and kids' activities. Sunday looked similar, just different tasks, but no actual rest. Guilt appeared whenever I sat still. I was physically present with my family, but my attention was divided and always pulled toward the next thing that needed done. By Sunday night, Monday felt like it was already here and I was already behind. They say you can tell a lot about your job by how you feel on Sunday night. I felt dread at the thought of another week in the same cycle.

This wasn't one particularly bad day; this was every day. The unsustainability wasn't dramatic, it was cumulative. The realization didn't arrive as crisis, but as a quiet certainty. I can't do this for five more years, but I also didn't know how to stop. The warrior knows how to push through exhaustion, but not how to rest. It knows how to work harder, but not how to work less. That's when the five-year plan started to form, not as escape, but as acknowledgment that something had to change, even if I didn't yet know what.

The monthly payments alone were enormous, roughly $3,200 every month, all from credit cards and a 401(k) loan. No mortgage or car payments, just debt tied directly to survival, transition, and maintenance. It had become as fixed and unquestioned as utilities or insurance. Something to manage, not escape. The debt had built up slowly and steadily.

I don't remember a specific moment when I first calculated that $3,200 total and thought, how did we get here? We knew how we got there. Medical expenses, the basement renovation, transitions between two divorces, a car purchase after my second divorce, and years' worth of regular everyday things that don't register individually.

None of it seemed reckless. It was all defensible, but defensible and sustainable are not the same thing. The shift from debt as emergency to debt as fixed cost happened gradually, masked by the fast pace of everyday life. There was no single moment when it became as fixed and unquestioned as utilities. It just absorbed itself into the structure. Another line item. Another obligation that required management but no longer demanded urgent action. That normalization was dangerous. Margin wasn't just not growing, the very thin margin we had was shrinking, and at times it was negative. This looked and felt exactly as I remembered in my childhood home, just with newer, bigger, and better "stuff".

We were one major disruption away from collapse. A job loss, a medical emergency, or a vehicle failure that couldn't be patched together cheaply would have felt catastrophic. There was no room to adjust, no slack to absorb a hit. Every dollar already had a job, and most of those jobs were defensive.

By then, our family had shifted again. Most of the kids were grown and gone. What had once been a full house was now just us and one teenager in a six-bedroom home. The space wasn't eerie or confusing; it was simply quieter, and somehow messier. And in that quiet, it became harder to ignore the cost of what it had taken to get here.

I was still pushing forward; harder, in fact. I was actively pursuing a director-level promotion, one that would bring more responsibility, more pressure, and more income. But at the same time, I was also quietly looking for another job altogether. Not for more money, but for peace. I pursued both simultaneously for about a year.

The contradiction of working toward a promotion at my current job while looking for another job didn't feel strange at the time. It felt logical. Emotionally, I had already checked out of my role. I would still show up, still do my best, and I still cared, but I knew I would not retire from this place or this career. It hadn't become short term yet, but it wasn't permanent in my mind anymore either.

It made perfect sense to me. I would either get more money or more peace. Both were attractive options, and I was willing to take whichever door opened first. I was looking for similar roles, leadership positions in healthcare technology or finance. Something that required the skills I had built but might offer a different environment with different pressures and different constraints.

I had one interview during that period that would have been a remote leadership role in healthcare technology. My salary requirement was above their range, and that was the deciding factor. The interview went very well, but I wasn't selected. Looking back, I'm not sure what I would have done if I had been, but I'm grateful I wasn't. In hindsight I would realize that it was a blessing that I wasn't offered that position. More on that soon.

Being promoted to director would have brought more income, yes, but it also would have locked me further into a system I was planning to leave eventually. The other job might have brought relief, but it also might have just been the same treadmill at a different incline. Either way I was looking for opportunities, but they just weren't appearing.

Both efforts were attempts to solve the same problem using the only tools I trusted, motion, advancement, and endurance. My wife and I began having conversations at home that would have been unthinkable years earlier. We talked about me leaving management. In fact, leaving healthcare entirely and teaching full-time.

My wife knew how much I loved teaching, so she wasn't surprised when I brought up the idea of doing it full-time. Not immediately, but in five years or so, maybe. Once the debt was manageable. Once the pressure eased enough to breathe. You know.... "someday".

The five-year timeline wasn't arbitrary, however. I did the calculations based on our current debt payoff schedule and any additional money we could add to it from my adjunct opportunities. She also had access to some overtime opportunities now, and with most of the kids already moved out, it was easier to do the extras. Looking at the payment schedule to get us to a place where it was possible, even if not necessarily comfortable, for me to transition into teaching full-time looked like a lifetime away and it would be a struggle. We wouldn't be able to let up at all for those five years. Anything that interfered with the payment plan would push us out that much further from the goal.

It was based on debt reduction projections and the point at which we could afford a likely drop in income without destabilizing everything we had built. Five years felt both possible and impossibly far away at the same time, but I believed it would happen. We were ready to commit to that plan and make it real instead of just aspirational. It wasn't a short-term pressure release valve; it was a long-term goal. At least, that's what I told myself.

Slowing down still felt risky. No longer because I was afraid of becoming poor again, but because I had no idea who I would be without constant motion. With the five-year plan, however, we wouldn't have to worry about slowing down anytime soon. To get where we needed to be, slowing down wasn't an option.

Workdays were long, and teaching meant travel, management meant constant availability, and even exercise was functional. Mowing the yard, carrying materials, fixing things myself because paying someone else felt irresponsible, even then.

There was no time for exercise that wasn't productive or necessary. I tried to build small things into my routine like always taking the stairs at work or parking a little farther away, but only what I could work into the regular flow of the day. Anything more than that felt impossible.

Traveling to teach classes made that even harder. During my busiest teaching schedule, I was driving to three different campuses, three days a week. All of them were over an hour away and it was common for me to get home after 10:30 p.m. on those nights. Even in a normal teaching week, I was making one or two commutes of forty-five to sixty minutes each way.

Once while watching Rocky IV with my wife, an image really stood out to me. There's a scene where the Russian boxer, Ivan Drago, is running on a treadmill and his trainers keep increasing the incline. I said, "That's how I feel most of the time." The image stuck with me. Running harder, working harder, but the treadmill keeps inclining. You're moving faster just to stay in the same place. How long can you keep that up? That visual was accurate in a way that felt uncomfortably precise.

I was good at this life. Exceptionally good, and that was the problem. I had built a system optimized for motion, not for recovery. For vigilance, not peace. For holding things together, not removing what made them fragile in the first place. This was the first danger zone. Not the one that comes after debt is gone, but the one before anything truly changes.

High income, high responsibility, high exhaustion, and all the competence to keep everything going. It's seductive here. You tell yourself this is just a demanding season and that things will ease once the next milestone is reached. Once the promotion

comes. Once the balance drops a little more.
Once the kids are fully launched. Once
there's time. Someday.

But the treadmill didn't get easier, it kept
inclining. I was still moving, but now I was
working harder to stay in the same place,
and without realizing it, I was approaching
the edge of something I hadn't planned for
at all.

There were no moments of clarity during
this period where I thought something has
to give. I just kept moving, because that's
what I have always done. The break came
anyway. Not because I chose it, but because
the system finally made the choice for me.

I didn't know it was coming. One week I was
still diligently planning my next five years
and the next week I was heading into my
boss's office for a meeting that I wasn't
completely confident about.

Chapter 7: Think It Can't Happen to You?

The healthcare system I worked for was having serious financial issues. Being a manager, I was included in talks about the budget strains and possible layoffs and was aware that I would be letting some of my own people go. Awareness stops at your own level, however.

I was scheduled for a meeting with my boss, the CIO. It was 8:00 a.m. on a Monday morning. August 7. The meeting invite had arrived the Friday before, which made the timing a little suspicious, but we had been discussing the director promotion frequently, so it didn't seem overly suspicious. My CIO had made it clear that he supported my promotion.

The meeting was also set up as a recurring event, which gave me some hope. I thought, why would he do that if I was being let go? It was the kind of absurd detail that you laugh about in hindsight.

The drive to work that morning was anxious. I spent the weekend running through scenarios. Promotion or termination. Advancement or elimination. Both felt equally possible, and I had no way to know which conversation I was walking into.

I was trying to play through both scenarios in my head, and it probably wasn't a safe drive being distracted the entire way.

My wife and I talked a lot about both possibilities that weekend. We tried to approach it logically, running through scenarios without letting the emotion take over. What would we do if it was a promotion? What would we do if it was termination? We mapped out both paths as if they were equally abstract and equally likely.

But the logic only worked in short bursts. Saturday afternoon felt manageable, but Saturday night the concern was louder. Sunday morning brought a different kind of weight that felt heavier. Whatever the outcome, something was about to shift.

We didn't argue and we weren't short with each other, but every conversation had an undercurrent. Every silence felt loaded. I'd catch myself staring at nothing, running the same mental loops. She'd ask if I was okay and I'd say yes, but neither of us believed it.

We didn't sleep well that weekend, which wasn't unusual for us during that period, but this was different. The air was heavier. Not tense, exactly, but more like very slow waiting with a lot of anticipation. Like standing in the parking lot before a storm arrives, knowing it's coming but not knowing when or how hard it will hit. Anticipation with a bit of a sharp edge.

By Sunday night I'd given up trying to guess. The meeting was twelve hours away now and I'd know soon enough. Not knowing seemed worse than either outcome would be, but at the same time, a deep and strange calm settled in me. I never told my wife, but I almost hoped I was being let go. At least in that scenario I didn't quit.

That is 100% warrior language. Always ready to fight but never willing to give up; and if I was simply let go, I could still say I fought and didn't give up. At this point, the unknown almost looked like a better option than continuing on my current path. It was very evident in my life that I needed a change, but that didn't help me sleep that night.

The walk from the parking lot to his office felt longer than usual. I kept my pace normal and deliberate. Not rushed, not hesitant. I was suddenly aware of my breathing and how tightly I was holding my shoulders.

My boss opened his office door after I knocked, and when I walked in, just to my right, my former director was seated at a small table. There were papers in front of her and more in front of the seat he would sit in. I read the room immediately. Their presence together, the tone, and some bit of my own intuition, there was no question.

I knew.

The same air I felt when I'd been on the other side of these conversations. The room has a particular weight when you're being let go. It's different from a performance review. Different from a promotion discussion. You can feel it before anyone says a word.

The answer settled over me, calm, clear, and unavoidable. I had hoped for the promotion conversation, but this one didn't surprise me. After 23 years I was being laid off.

It wasn't performance-related, and it wasn't personal, it was pure economics. I knew the numbers, and I knew the logic. The system was cutting five percent of its workforce, roughly five hundred people overall. This included about twenty percent of management positions, stretching all the way up to the C-suite. I wasn't being singled out, just part of a calculation. That knowledge helped, but only slightly.

The conversation was calm and direct, but also sincere and personal. My CIO explained that he knew I understood the hospital's financial situation and that layoffs were happening across the organization. Then he said it very plainly "Unfortunately, you're part of the five percent who are being released."

I acknowledged this immediately and told them I wasn't surprised. The strategy made sense. I was at the upper end of the manager's pay scale, and I knew I would be replaced with someone earning less. That's standard procedure in a workforce reduction. Positions are either eliminated entirely or replaced with cheaper labor.

We hugged. My director hugged me. There were tears, mine and theirs. I'm sure it wasn't easy for them either. I worked very closely with both of them for many years and they both supported my various roles and promotions. We didn't always agree on things, and some things we absolutely disagreed on, but we had meaningful history together and we successfully built a very large and complex system.

They offered me the choice to finish the week at home, disengaged, or I could stay and wrap things up with care. I didn't hesitate. I told them immediately that I would stay to transition my responsibilities, hold my meetings, inform my peers and colleagues, and leave everything as supported as possible. Maintaining my dignity mattered to me.

After going back into the office the next day, I called a meeting with my team, who I assumed had already heard the news. That kind of thing travels very fast. I told them the reality of the situation, and that the layoffs included me. I explained that I would continue to work over the next week to hand off work and close out as many tasks as possible, and that they would be in good hands and would continue to do well in the organization. They were mostly quiet, some in disbelief, and many came to my office individually to express their concern and condolences.

After the meeting with my team, I walked back to my office and gathered a few personal items. I didn't have many personal items at work. I'd been in that role for years, but I'd never been someone who decorated or accumulated things. A few framed certificates, a mug, and some files I'd need to hand off properly over the next week.

The building felt different walking through it after that. Not hostile, but unfamiliar. Like I was already gone even though I was still technically there. Colleagues I passed in the hallway looked at me with a mix of sympathy and relief. Sympathy because it was me, and relief because it wasn't them.

I nodded. Kept moving. Held it together.

Although I chose to stay and finish my week,
that day after being informed of my
termination, I went home. When I got to my
car, I sat in the driver's seat for a moment
before starting it. Not processing, exactly,
just breathing. The weekend's anxiety was
gone and replaced by something cleaner,
certainly. The decision had been made. The
uncertainty was over, and now there was
just the path forward, and I was already
thinking about what that looked like.

Just nine days earlier, before I learned of
layoffs coming, I had bought a truck. A
Chevy Colorado, not excessive, not a full-
size truck, just reasonable and new. It was
the first brand new vehicle I had ever owned
in my life. I was forty-nine years old.

The 2011 Ford Escape I'd been driving was
starting to have transmission issues. It had
over 200,000 miles on it, was twelve years
old, and I was still driving to distant
campuses to teach and travelling between 3
different office locations for my
management job. My wife and I talked
about it. The promotion seemed imminent,
the income was stable, and it was time.

It felt exciting, not excessive. A modest
upgrade after years of making do. Nine days
later, walking out of that building, one
thought kept surfacing through everything

else. I'm keeping that truck. The warrior in me had already decided that whatever it took, I was not losing that truck. I'd work three jobs if I had to. I'd cut everything else. But that truck, the first new vehicle I'd ever owned, was mine, and I was going to keep it.

Looking back, that reaction tells you everything you need to know about the warrior identity. I didn't think, "Do I still need this truck?" Instead, I thought, "How do I defend what's mine?"

But that day, I went home. I wasn't stunned; I was invigorated. I called my wife as soon as I left the office. She was much more upset than I was; scared, I'm sure. We had talked all weekend about the possibility that the meeting could go either way, but I think she genuinely believed I was going to be offered the promotion.

She was at work, so we didn't get to talk for long. I just wanted her to hear it from me and quickly, since as I said, that kind of news gets around fast and she worked for the same health system by then. She had started there just a month earlier. I reiterated that I had options and that I would start working on a plan as soon as I got home. She was quiet and on the verge of tears. Her voice was shaky. I didn't want her to worry, but she was going to worry no matter what I said. How could she not? How could I not?

I can't say there was an absence of fear for me. It was there, but it wasn't an overriding feeling. What I felt most was relief. Relief to finally know the outcome after an anxious weekend. Relief that the uncertainty was over, and underneath that, I felt something unexpected. Momentum. The decision had been made for me, and whether I was ready or not, a major change was at my doorstep. There was no reason to dwell on what had happened. The path forward was the only thing that mattered now, and as I always did, I got to work on a solution immediately.

By 10:00 a.m., I was on the phone. I reached out to a former professor from my MBA program. Not with any grand plan or expectations, just a question. Were there any additional teaching opportunities available? Was there anything I could pick up to stabilize things while I figured out what came next? Fall semester was only a few weeks away, and that fact suddenly mattered.

It was pure action mode and whether I wanted to or not, I had to put the shock of it all on hold and get busy on a plan. I had a very good relationship with this professor; he was one of my favorites during my MBA time and just a great person all around. I knew if something was available, he would point me to it.

I told him the facts that I had just been informed of my layoff and that I had one week of employment left, then I asked about the adjunct opportunities. He said there weren't any adjunct needs he was aware of at the moment, but then he paused and said, "There may be something else. Let me call you back." I had no idea what he meant. It sounded positive, but I really had no clue.

When he called back it wasn't about adjunct work. Instead, he was connecting me with a local college that urgently needed a full-time business professor. Without one, they would have to cancel some fall classes, so they needed someone immediately. That same day, on Monday, I was able to speak with the department chair. The next day I was called back and invited for an interview to be held that Friday.

The interview was straightforward. They asked about my degree and professional background and teaching experience. Fortunately, my teaching experience was extensive after 12 years of adjunct teaching at a full-time equivalent load. I emphasized the wide variety of course titles I had taught across seven different institutions and my history of strong teaching evaluations. I also mentioned that I was already familiar with their learning management system, which meant I could hit the ground running.

Some unfamiliar things struck me during the interview. It wasn't held in a typical uninspiring office environment; we met for dinner. The interview included the department chair and three other professors on the faculty search committee. There were no canned interview questions that sounded like they were rehearsed from an HR manual, just natural, relaxed conversation. The tone of it all felt so foreign from the environment I'd been accustomed to. It was very welcoming.

They were appreciative of my sudden availability, but more than that I think they were relieved. I was offered the job on the following Monday, just one week since I had made the call looking for adjunct opportunities. The contract arrived on Tuesday, which also happened to be my final day of employment at the health system. It felt surreal. Lucky. Like many things had aligned in a way I couldn't have orchestrated myself. The timing was perfect for me and for them. I had about ten days between being hired and the start of the semester. Just enough time for someone who was quite used to delivering on a short runway.

For the next four months I was receiving severance pay while also earning full-time income from my new employer. On top of that I had over three hundred hours of paid time-off that I would receive and a pension payout I had forgotten existed. It didn't erase the debt, but it created some margin, and it created momentum. For the first time, we had something resembling choice.

When I realized the leverage this scenario provided, the conversation with my wife was now filled with gratitude rather than fear. Not relief in the sense of "now we can finally breathe", but gratitude in the sense of "we've been given an unexpected gift, and we know exactly what to do with it."

There was never any discussion about doing anything else with the extra money. No vacations. No upgrades. No rewards for making it through. Every dollar would go toward the debt. It wasn't a hard decision; it was the obvious one. We felt like we had been blessed with an incredible and unexpected situation, and the only strategic response was to use it exactly as it needed to be used.

I calculated everything as I always did. The income overlap wouldn't eliminate our debt entirely, but it would significantly reduce the load. It would shorten the debt payoff timeline by about three years. That

mattered in a huge way. For the first time in
a long time, the math was working in our
favor, and for the first time in decades, I
wasn't fighting just to stay in place. I was
moving forward with intention.

Chapter 8: The Tired Warrior

For years my life had been calibrated to motion. Long days of overlapping roles. Teaching layered on top of management. Always on call to something or someone. And even though rest had a purpose, it only existed to refuel me just enough to keep going. Now, suddenly, the pace had changed.

I was no longer managing a department. I was no longer accountable to a constant stream of emails, meetings, and after-hours decision support and crisis calls. I was teaching full-time, something I had already been doing in practice for years, but now it was my only professional role, and it felt almost surreal. What surprised me the most was the sudden free time. Margin now existed in a space it never had before.

When I first learned what "full-time" meant in higher education, I was genuinely shocked. I even giggled about it. The course load, the expectations, the structure. I had already been teaching at or above a full-time load for nearly a decade on top of a demanding management career, but no one had ever told me that. Suddenly, I wasn't filling time with busy work. I wasn't proving presence for its own sake. I was being paid to think, prepare and deliver content, mentor students, and change lives in a profound and meaningful way.

As a manager, I hated the façade of productivity. I hated the idea that a person could be viewed as unproductive if they did their work efficiently, while a less efficient person is viewed as productive simply because they're always "busy". I used to say that "Time on Teams is not a measure of productivity", which was not a perspective necessarily shared by my own leadership. That environment was behind me now, and suddenly there were gaps in my day. Big gaps. In fact, I was only "at work" four days a week with every Wednesday off. This was a huge change in my schedule. The first week was unsurprisingly comfortable. The classes I taught were familiar, and the schedule felt light. Full-time at this college meant three classes, and there was no requirement for me to be on campus on my Wednesday off.

At first, I thought, this can't be right. I had no idea what to do with those first few Wednesdays. I felt guilty, like I should be doing something, like there was work I was missing or obligations I was neglecting. The absence of pressure felt suspicious, but I wasn't missing anything. The work was getting done, and there was no pressure to "appear" busy.

I don't even know what I actually did that first Wednesday off. It's still a blur. I was likely pouring over the budget or fretting over the details of the severance, PTO, and pension payout schedules to be sure our plan was sound. Despite the welcome change, my posture had not yet relaxed.

I spent a lot of that early time going through institutional policies and learning about my new workplace and colleagues. I frequently had wonderful, relaxed, often deep conversations with my peers. The kind of conversations that weren't forced, transactional or rushed. Conversations that went places naturally.

A professor who had an office right next to mine used to stop just for social conversation. He was a deep thinker and very smart. Not that the people I used to work with weren't smart, they were, but academics think differently, and I really enjoyed those conversations. They're challenging and push you out of your lane a bit.

I loved being in an academic environment. I still do. A few weeks in, something unexpected started to happen. Free thinking and creativity began to occupy my time. Ideas that weren't tied to solving an immediate problem, managing a crisis, or implementing strategy. Thoughts arrived simply because there was space for them.

That space was new; real space and time to sit and think. Time to read without multitasking. Time to walk without an agenda. Time that didn't need to be monetized or justified.

At first that stillness felt uncomfortable. I realized how deeply conditioned I had become to urgency. I still monitored the budget closer than ever, even as the numbers improved. Any unexpected expense still triggered concern. Every deviation felt like something that needed immediate attention. The danger had passed, but my nervous system hadn't gotten the memo.

The vigilance still showed up mentally, but physically things started to change. I was still in reactive mode, still listening for alerts from my phone at night, even though there was no longer a system that could go down. I still had trouble sleeping and I still woke up to the slightest sound. The hypervigilance didn't stop just because the circumstances had changed, but physically I began to feel much better. I was lighter, slower, and more grounded. I walked for myself, for my health, without a destination and without urgency. I spent time outside with and without purpose, but even when it was with purpose, it was simply to enjoy the fresh air and maybe see and feel a bit of nature.

It wasn't until about 6 months later that I truly relaxed at night before going to sleep. There was one night in particular that I remember turning my phone's ringer off. I thought at the time that it was symbolic in some way, like giving myself permission to detach from it. Of course I told my wife I was doing this in case any family emergency came up, she would be getting the call, not me. See, even though I was actively breaking this habit, I was still preparing! The warrior was still present and in charge.

We aren't meant to live forever in a state of high alert. What I was beginning to feel then, slowly and unevenly, was a sort of fatigue that I didn't quite understand. I didn't hate my work, I loved it. I wasn't disengaged; I was more engaged than ever, and I wasn't lost. I was just finally aware of the cost of carrying everything for so long, and for the first time, I had the space to notice it. This was the first time I felt my shoulders drop and was able to take a long, deep, actual and metaphorical breath. The fatigue wasn't from work; it was from release.

I didn't consciously label that identity as a "warrior" until much later. The language came from conversations with my wife, where I described our struggles as a constant fight; one we had fought long and hard. The warrior framing only became clear during a period of reflection when I finally had time to sit and think abstractly.

I realized that my life was moving through three archetypes. The warrior, then the keeper, and eventually, the sage. The shift from warrior to keeper wasn't sudden. It was gradual, and I suspected that I wasn't the only person who related to these transitions.

It took about a full year before I let myself relax into the stillness. It was also about that long before I finally regularly slept without anticipating a call in the middle of the night. The nervous system moves slower than circumstances do. I had maintained a warrior identity out of necessity for most of my life, and it had served me well. It helped me survive poverty, build a career, raise a family, and shoulder responsibilities that often felt heavier than I was ready for.

The formal connection to my past career ended in August, but the emotional connection remained for much longer.

For over a year after the layoff, I still said "we" when talking about my former employer. Not "they "or "them", but "we", as if I was still working there. As if twenty-three years of connection could not be severed cleanly by a termination conversation and a severance package.

I'd catch myself mid-sentence. "We're implementing a new system" and then stop. No, they are, not we. I don't work there anymore. The correction felt awkward every time, like learning to write with my non-dominant hand.

Former colleagues still reached out regularly. Many of them wanted to complain about how things have been going since the restructuring. How the new systems weren't working well. How the team dynamics had shifted and some things were falling apart without the people who'd been let go.

I didn't want to enjoy those conversations, but if I'm being honest, I did. It was validating in a twisted way. Proof that my presence mattered and that my contributions weren't so easily replaceable. That the decision to eliminate my position had consequences.

The warrior in me fed on that validation, but the keeper knew it wasn't healthy.

My wife still works there. That adds another layer of complexity I didn't anticipate. She talks about work and about people I used to interact with daily, and about systems I helped build from nothing. In some ways she has inherited part of my network; twenty-three years of relationships that didn't disappear just because I was no longer there.

I hope she takes full advantage of that. It deserves to live on after that much time and energy spent developing it. But it's strange to be on the outside of something I helped create. Hearing about it secondhand and no longer part of the "we" I instinctively still wanted to claim.

Over time I also noticed I wasn't engaging with the budget as heavily or as often. I let receipts pile up for a few days, which I never would have done before. I moved payments to autopay, something I had resisted for years because I didn't want to give up that control, but now I wanted systems that didn't require constant monitoring. I wanted to stop thinking about it so much and I was ready to trust the process. That's when it settled on me that I could relax my posture.

I grieved the warrior's identity. In some ways, I still do. It had been my identity for my entire adult life. Letting it go felt uncomfortable and I still fight feelings of laziness or wastefulness when I pay for things I wouldn't have before, like buying new things, name-brand things, and paying for services that I had always performed myself. Those things still felt very unfamiliar.

The warrior had kept me alive, but he was tired, and slowly, I was learning that survival and living aren't the same thing. With that space came something unexpected, even more creativity. Ideas surfaced that had been buried for years under obligation. I began thinking not just about what I could do next, but who I wanted to be. Not as a provider or problem-solver, but as a person. What had my identity been? What is it now? What do I want it to become? That's when I had thought that would have been impossible before. The idea of earning a PhD was finally realistic.

I was standing at the edge of something I never imagined would be possible, pursuing the highest academic degree available. And in a turn of irony that still gives me pause, the field was Personal Financial Planning. The very subject that had shaped my life through struggle, adaptation, and hard-earned understanding.

For the first time, the constraints that had always governed my decisions, time and money, were no longer immovable barriers, they were just variables to manage. The idea had surfaced in conversations with my wife long before I lost my job, but not as being even remotely possible. There was no money and no time for something like that. It felt like something that existed far down the road, if at all. I had even discussed this with the dean of the university I was teaching as an adjunct and would later go on to teach full-time, but at the time it was more of a dream than reality.

It finally became real about a year after I started teaching full-time, and around the same time that I began to relax my posture.

Choosing Personal Financial Planning for my PhD work wasn't as ironic as it sounds. It was the perfect choice and where my real passion lives. I had been advising people for a few years by then, and I genuinely love personal finance. All of it. Investing, taxes, budgets, retirement planning, the mechanics and the meaning of it. But more than anything I have a deep interest in our behavior around money and identity, and I wanted to research those intersections.

My interest in personal finance started during my MBA. I loved the economics and finance classes I took. They asked questions that mattered to me, and the integration of those concepts changes our lives in a material way. The piece that was missing, however, is the behavior behind it all.

The PhD interested me for other reasons as well. From a personal perspective, it was the academic finish line. The validation of an arc that had started thirty-four years ago at just seventeen years old in a small community college, working night shift at a grocery store just to barely afford tuition. It was a promise to my mom and grandmother kept.

Both my mom and grandmother always believed in me without fail, and they told me this often. I also have a great-aunt who made me feel like nothing was impossible for me. Other family members encouraged and supported me as well. I never told my mom or grandmother that I intended to get a PhD because that didn't even become a thought until after they had both passed, but I did tell them that I would keep going, whatever that meant.

I knew early in my adult life that whatever I had to go through to escape the poverty I grew up in might not significantly benefit me directly. It might not change my own life in the ways people imagine when they talk about "making it", and that was okay. My intention was never really about me; it was about changing outcomes for my kids and the generations that would follow them. I wanted to be a generational shield for them, so that when they looked back, they would not be burdened by what came before.

I never expected to be wealthy or particularly comfortable. I just wanted them to have a shot at comfort that I never had in their material lives and in their mental and emotional lives. One that didn't require the kind of endurance and sacrifice that had defined my own path. That was my purpose, and it drove everything, even when I couldn't see the finish line.

From a professional perspective, I wanted to engage in research that asked questions about poverty and identity. About post-poverty and post-debt identity crisis. About experiences and patterns that I had lived and was beginning to understand. The conversation with my wife was full of support. She was excited and in many ways, she has been my biggest cheerleader, fully believing in me even when I struggled to believe in myself.

There was no longer a concern about time or cost. Not anymore. The margin was fully internalized by then, and we were ready to move ahead.

After I applied to the program I was interviewed and accepted, and then reality hit me. I really could do this. This would not be a process of razor-thin margin, but a planned, comfortable path.

I went through the graduate certificate program in Personal Financial Planning first, as a prerequisite for the PhD. It was a good test of the time and money pressures, and after that, we were very comfortable with the decision to move forward. That didn't mean everything was always easy, or calm, or resolved, but it meant the pace could finally change.

As the warrior rested, something else began to emerge. Not all at once, not cleanly, but quietly. What exactly was emerging wasn't clear at the time. It would take more free thinking to name the identity as the "keeper". That language came later, through more reflection and distance just as the warrior identity had been recognized.

In my classrooms something was shifting. Something had already shifted. Teaching full-time without the management load layered on top changed how I taught and what I cared about in the classroom. As an adjunct, it was unlikely that I would ever encounter the same students again beyond those few classes. The relationship was transactional, even if it was meaningful at that moment. As a full-time professor, I was mentoring, advising, and engaging with some of the same students all the way through to graduation. I was facilitating their growth during a powerful time in their lives.

That personal fulfillment is further extended by students who stay in touch on LinkedIn and occasionally reach out for advice or just to say hi well after graduation. I've written many reference letters for students pursuing jobs or advanced degrees. It's extremely rewarding to give back in ways that others have given to me. It's also nice just to hear from them occasionally, casually.

It was much deeper engagement, and it mattered to me in a way the earlier work hadn't. I wasn't just delivering content anymore; I was investing in people and in their futures. In outcomes I may not see for years, and maybe never. That shift, from managing systems to shaping lives, felt significant. It required a different part of me. A part that hadn't been asked to show up before.

The warrior had been trained to fight, to endure, and to hold things together under pressure. The keeper was showing me something else. How to build, how to protect, how to set boundaries, and how to let things grow without forcing them. It was quieter work, slower work. For the first time in my life, that felt like enough. But it wasn't just enough, it was exactly right.

Disconnecting.

I had taken a laptop with me on a trip to Belize just under a year before I was let go from my job. I told my director that I did not intend to take my laptop or be available and asked if she would cover for me during that time. She knew that I never took vacations, and even during the long weekends I occasionally took, I remained available. She agreed, and that was the first time I was truly disconnected and disengaged from work in 20 years since becoming a systems engineer, and then manager. In hindsight, that felt like a very, very long time to remain engaged at that level, but still, the laptop went with me.

Ironically, the trip to Belize wasn't even a true vacation. I went there as a business consultant for a resort hotel, but during the non-business hours I was able to do many "vacation" things, and it was a wonderful trip. Oh, and that trip was just me and my mother-in-law, so you know I wasn't just a warrior, but I was a brave warrior! All kidding aside, she had a relationship with the resort owners and that is how I found myself there consulting them on their business strategy. I also enjoyed getting to know my mother-in-law.

In my new career, however, where I didn't need to make special arrangements to have a break, the next time I traveled would be less than a month after starting the fall semester when we went to Florida for our daughter's wedding. I could not think of any reason why I would need to bring a laptop, so I didn't. Still, this was way too early in the process for me to really feel comfortable without it and all the what-if scenarios were playing in my head. I think the first time I was away from home without it and didn't feel bothered by it was the next summer when we went to visit our oldest daughter, who by then lived in Iowa. It didn't even occur to me that I didn't take it until we got back home, and I told my wife that I hadn't missed it. I kind of just forgot about it. That was a "moment" for sure.

Expansion: The First Semester

The first few weeks at the college felt like stepping into a different world. Not just a different job, but a different way of existing professionally.

I had been teaching as an adjunct for years, always arriving just in time for class and leaving immediately after. I never lingered on campus. There was no time to build relationships with colleagues, and no space to engage with students beyond classroom hours. Teaching had been something I loved but squeezed into the spaces of an already overloaded life.

Now, suddenly, I had an office. A real office with my name on the door. A space that was mine, where I could sit and think and prepare without also monitoring my phone for work emergencies or calculating how many minutes I had before I needed to be somewhere else.

The department welcomed me warmly. These weren't people I was competing with for resources or navigating political dynamics around. They were genuinely glad I was there. We had sincere conversations about teaching philosophy, about students, about ideas, about life. Conversations that went deeper than logistics and deadline coordination and weren't rushed.

That first semester I taught three classes. Marketing, Accounting, and Financial Management. These weren't all the classes I wanted to focus on long-term, but they were a way in. I would have taught anything they needed to make this career transition work. Regardless, I was fully focused on providing the best classroom experience possible. The classrooms were new, the students were new, the environment and culture were new, but none of that matters when everyone shares a common goal and work ethic. It felt comfortable in a way I had never felt in my professional career.

But something also shifted in how I taught. As an adjunct, I had been organized, prepared, and effective, but there was always an edge of simple performance to it. I was proving I belonged. Proving I was worth hiring again. Now, with stability underneath me, I could focus entirely on the students. On whether they were actually learning, not just whether I was delivering content well.

I started lingering after class, not rushing out. Students would stay to ask questions, and for the first time in years, I had the margin to engage those questions fully. To follow tangents that mattered to them and have conversations that couldn't be scheduled or contained in neat blocks.

One student, I'll call him Marcus, came to my office during the second week. He was working full-time overnight at a warehouse and taking four classes. He looked exhausted in a way I recognized immediately.

He wanted advice on whether to take out student loans or keep working himself to exhaustion trying to pay as he went. I saw myself at twenty in him. The same belief that debt was failure. The same conviction that struggle proved commitment.

I didn't tell him what to do, but I did tell him my story. About working two jobs through nursing school. About the cost of that approach, not just financially, but physically, relationally. About how I had confused endurance with virtue for most of my life.

I wanted him to understand that sometimes life has sprints and sometimes it has marathons, but to be careful not to let a sprint become a marathon. That it was ok to endure now, but he should recognize that it should only meet a temporary necessity, not become a lifestyle. I didn't push him to continue his current path but just helped him recognize that an identity was at work and that identities can and should change when the circumstances allow it.

I never would have had that conversation as an adjunct. There wouldn't have been time, and even if there had been time, I wouldn't have had the emotional space to be that honest or that vulnerable. But the keeper was starting to emerge in me, and the keeper could be present in ways the warrior never could.

The overlap period when I was receiving severance while also earning a full salary created something I'd never experienced before; financial breathing room that finally felt permanent, not temporary. For the first four months of that first semester, every dollar of my severance went directly toward debt while my new salary covered our living expenses, but we could see the numbers changing in a way that always felt out of our reach. We were no longer thinking in terms of "someday".

It wasn't financial abundance in the way most people might imagine. We weren't taking vacations or buying new cars, but the pressure had fundamentally changed. The abundance we had then was felt, if not seen. For the first time in my adult life, an unexpected expense didn't trigger immediate stress. The furnace breaking or the car needing repairs were suddenly just inconvenient, not catastrophic.

My wife noticed the change before I did. One evening, maybe six weeks into the new job, she said, "You seem different. Lighter."

I hadn't realized it until she said it, but she was right. The constant low-grade tension that had been my baseline for decades was starting to ease. It wasn't gone, not even close, but easing. Around the same time, I had also lost about twenty more pounds. Not because I was dieting and trying to, but because meals no longer had to be fast and convenient. I took time to prepare better foods and had the space to enjoy meals. This was further enhanced by the severe decrease in daily stress, which keeps your cortisol levels high and fights your metabolism every minute of the day.

The warrior was still very-much present that first semester. I still checked my bank balance multiple times a day. I still tracked every expense. I still occasionally had dreams about being back at the hospital, systems failing, or people depending on me and me not being able to respond. But slowly, incrementally, new patterns were forming. The keeper was learning to trust what the warrior never could, that the systems would hold without constant monitoring. That rest wasn't dangerous. That enough was truly enough.

Learning to Stop Performing Availability

One of the earliest keeper behaviors I had to learn was letting go of performative availability. In my previous role, there was enormous pressure to appear constantly accessible. Microsoft Teams wasn't just a communication tool; it was a surveillance mechanism. Your status indicator mattered. "Available" or "Busy" was expected. "Away" was noticed. "Offline" often required explanation.

I had internalized this completely. I would artificially engage with my laptop just to keep my Teams status green anytime I had unscheduled time. Move the mouse. Type a few characters. Anything to prevent the system from marking me as away. Even when I was working on something offline, even when I stepped away to eat lunch or use the restroom, the pressure to be present online was constant. That is not healthy, physically or mentally.

The new environment didn't operate that way at all. Teams existed, but it wasn't weaponized. Many colleagues simply forgot to open the app in the morning. If someone needed you and you weren't available on Teams, they'd send an email, or walk to your office, or call your phone. There was no surveillance or judgment about your digital presence. If you were "away" or not on Teams at all, it was no big deal.

For the first few weeks, I still opened Teams first thing every morning out of habit. I still monitored my status and still felt that low-level pressure when I stepped away. But gradually, I noticed that nothing bad happened when I didn't. No one questioned my commitment. No one tracked my movements. My work was evaluated by outcomes, not by how green my status indicator stayed.

One morning, a few months in, I realized I had been working for a few hours before I even thought about Teams. I had been preparing for class, reviewing student work, responding to emails, doing meaningful work without once checking whether I appeared "available" to a system that wasn't watching.

That small shift represented something larger. The keeper was learning that availability should be based on reality, not virtual performance. That my value wasn't measured in constant accessibility. That boundaries around my time and attention weren't unprofessional, they were healthy and respected.

I also found myself working on things during the day that had nothing to do with my teaching responsibilities, like early dissertation ideas, reading for personal development, or projects that interested me but weren't directly tied to any immediate deliverable. Or simply enjoying some quiet time.

In my previous role, that would have been unthinkable. Every minute had to be accounted for, justified, productive in ways that were visible to others. But here, the expectation was different. As long as my classes were prepared, my students were supported, and my responsibilities were met, how I spent the rest of my time, even in my faculty office, was mine to determine.

The keeper could work on meaningful things without performing productivity. The warrior had never known that was possible.

Walking Without Destination

Another keeper practice that emerged was walking. Not functional exercise, like mowing the lawn or fixing something. Not walking to get somewhere specific, just walking for the sake of walking.

The campus was beautiful. There were old trees, open spaces, paths that wound between buildings. I started taking walks during my breaks between classes with no specific destination, no agenda, just moving through space with my thoughts.

This was radically different from how I'd moved through the world before. Every step in my previous life had purpose. You walked to get from point A to point B as efficiently as possible. You didn't waste time wandering. At best, at my former office building people walked around the parking lot. Trees were placed by design, not by nature. The traffic noise was constant. That does nothing for me, and even if I had the time I wouldn't have wanted to be in that over-processed environment.

But these walks around campus didn't waste time, they were time to think and time to recover. Time when ideas surfaced that had been buried under the constant noise of urgency. I would notice things like the way light filtered through leaves, the changing seasons, students gathered on benches, the rhythm of campus life.

One day during one of these walks, I noticed a large, bright orange mushroom growing out of a tree trunk. Chicken of the Woods, which is a choice edible mushroom I'd foraged for occasionally years ago when I had time for such things. Thick, healthy, and absolutely beautiful!

I stood there looking at it, genuinely delighted. Not because of the mushroom itself, though it was impressive, but because I had the mental space and time to stop to notice it. The old version of me would have walked right past, head down, already thinking about the next obligation. This version could stop, appreciate my find, and email the grounds supervisor to ask if I could harvest it (she gave me an enthusiastic, yes). The next day I took it home, prepared it, cooked it, and enjoyed it...slowly.

That mushroom became symbolic for me of what margin can create. Not just financial breathing room, but the capacity to be present. to notice, and to engage with the world around you in ways that have nothing to do with productivity or obligation.

I still take those walks. Other times I just stand at my office window and look outside, watching the campus move through its day.

Before, I would have seen this as wasted time. Now I know it's necessary time that creates space for the kind of thinking and being that can't happen when you're always racing.

Eating with Colleagues

Another shift happened around lunch. As a manager and adjunct, I ate quickly, usually alone, at my desk and often in my car between obligations. Food was fuel, consumed as efficiently as possible before rushing to the next thing.

Now I am eating lunch with colleagues in the cafeteria or sometimes off campus. Not every day, but regularly. Meals meant to enjoy, not just refueling stops. Engaging in conversations that have nothing to do with work but everything to do with connection.

We talk about books we're reading, about our families, about ideas that interest us, and often about nothing in particular. The content didn't matter, but the presence did.

These lunches aren't scheduled or structured. They happen organically when schedules aligned and someone says, "I'm heading to grab lunch, want to come?" and I can say yes without calculating what I'd have to sacrifice to make the time.

That difference, between function and relation, marked another small shift in how I was learning to exist in the world.

The PhD Decision: A Keeper's Choice

The decision to pursue a PhD represents a fundamental shift in how I approached education and credentials.

Every degree before this one had been tactical. Nursing because it led to employment. Computer science because it enabled advancement. The MBA because it prepared me for leadership. Each one was a tool for something else. Each one was leveraged for promotion, for income, for the next step up the ladder.

The PhD is different. It comes with a major credential, yes, but not one I plan to leverage into anything specific. There's no promotion I'm chasing. No employer offering tuition reimbursement. No external pressure or timeline. This is entirely for me and my family, paid for by me, at my pace, and for my reasons. It also allows me to add something meaningful to the world through research without expecting anything in return.

That shift felt significant. Before, I collected credentials as armor. More education meant more protection, more options, and more expected safety. Now I pursue education from curiosity and genuine interest. Not to prove anything, not to leverage anything, just to learn and to give.

I'm not racing toward completion. There is no artificial deadline. I work on my coursework when I have time and energy. I engage deeply with material that interests me, and I allow myself to follow tangents that matter to me even when they don't directly serve the degree requirements.

This was the keeper setting boundaries. I did not allow external pressures to share this with me. I did not structure it to serve someone else's timeline or expectations. I was moving at my pace, with my own compass. That autonomy felt unfamiliar at first, almost suspicious, but gradually it became comfortable.

I no longer needed every achievement to justify itself through external validation. I could pursue something simply because it mattered to me. That difference between external validation and internal meaning marked the shift more clearly than anything else.

When the Warrior Reasserted Itself

The transition from warrior to keeper isn't linear. There were days, sometimes weeks, when I slipped back into old patterns without even noticing.

The debt was winding down, but slowly. We had started with an enormous balance that was over $107,000 in revolving credit card debt plus the 401(k) loan. Even with the severance overlap creating unprecedented progress, in the early stages the balance still seemed impossibly large. The numbers moved, but it moved in increments that felt insignificant against the total.

During those early months, I was still reacting to the budget every day. Multiple times a day usually. I would check balances, review transactions, recalculate projections. The spreadsheet was always open. The numbers were always in my head. Even though I had a clear payment plan and could see the progress mapped out month by month, old patterns still controlled the household budget.

There were also moments when unexpected expenses would trigger the full warrior response. The furnace failed one winter morning. Not a small repair; it needed to be replaced entirely, a significant expense and something I couldn't do myself.

Rationally, I knew we could handle it. We finally had emergency savings. We had margin. This was exactly the kind of thing margin is designed to absorb. But at that moment, I felt the old panic rise up. The immediate mental scramble. Where will the money come from? What do we need to cut? How far will this set us back?

I caught myself doing the warrior math again, calculating the payment amount, the minimum viable replacement cost, could we patch it rather than truly fix it. My wife saw this happening.

"We're replacing it," she said. "We're not patching it and we're not buying the cheapest option that might fail again in a few years. We're getting a good one, having it installed properly, and moving on."

She was right, but it took me a few days to settle into that reality. To stop running scenarios in my head, and to trust that one expense wasn't going to unravel everything we'd built.

The warrior also reasserted itself in my work habits, even in the new environment. There were stretches where I would over-commit and say yes to extra projects, volunteer for committees, take on more than my load required. Not because the job demanded it, but because I still equated motion with value.

One semester I agreed to teach an overload course, develop a new curriculum for another program, serve on two committees, and take on an advisee load that was higher than typical for a new faculty member. None of this was required, but all of it was offered, and I accepted everything.

About halfway through that semester, I felt exhaustion creeping in again. Not the bone-deep, system-wide exhaustion of my previous career, but tired in a way that felt familiar and wrong. I was slipping back into the belief that if I wasn't running at capacity, I wouldn't be doing enough. I felt the challenge of how much I can maintain at once, even though that was no longer necessary.

A colleague noticed and during a casual conversation in the hallway, he asked how things were going.

"Busy," I said. "But good."

He paused, looked at me with genuine concern. "You know you don't have to do all of that, right? You're new. You're allowed to say no."

I kind of chuckled. I did know that, but knowing and practicing are different things.

That conversation stayed with me. The keeper was learning, slowly, that enough was a real threshold. That I didn't have to fill every available hour just because hours were available. That rest wasn't something to earn, it was something to protect. Later there was an invitation to participate in something I was more than capable of, but I wouldn't have been able to give it appropriate time or attention. I simply said thanks, but no. There was no judgment, no raised eyebrows. It was just accepted. What a strange feeling.

The resistance to change wasn't dramatic. There was no crisis moment where I almost destroyed what I'd built. It was subtler than that. It was the daily habit of checking the budget obsessively even when there was nothing to check. It was the reflexive "yes" to every opportunity even when saying no was the healthier answer. It was the tension that immediately surfaced when anything deviated from the plan, even when the plan had room for deviation.

The warrior had kept me going for over thirty years of my adult life. That identity wasn't going to disappear just because circumstances had changed. It was going to linger, assert itself, and test whether the new way of being was really safe.

The keeper's work during this period wasn't just building new patterns. It was recognizing when the old patterns resurfaced and then consciously choosing differently, again and again, until slowly, incrementally, the new way began to feel more natural than the old.

Chapter 9: Becoming the Keeper

The debt didn't disappear all at once, it receded slowly. It took two more years to pay off the remaining balances. From the moment the severance overlap began to the day the last balance hit zero, two full years of disciplined, relentless focus. Every dollar from the overlap went toward debt. Then, after that window closed, we stayed committed. No backsliding. No reward spending. Just steady, intentional progress, but from a much different place emotionally and mentally.

The Final Year

The last twelve months of debt payoff felt different from all the months before. Not easier, exactly, but purposeful in a way that the earlier grinding hadn't been.

For the first time, I could see the finish line. Not the abstract "someday", but an actual date on the calendar. Based on our payment schedule and the remaining balance, I knew that barring any major disruption, we would be debt-free by early November.

That timeline became both motivating and dangerous. Motivating because every payment visibly moved the needle, each month to a greater degree. The balance dropped from five figures to four. Then from mid-four figures to low-four figures. Each month the numbers got smaller in ways that felt meaningful, not incremental.

But dangerous because the closer we got, the more tempting it became to ease up. To justify one purchase that "wouldn't really matter". To celebrate early and treat ourselves for making it this far.

We didn't do that, but the temptation was real, and it showed me something important about how debt traps work, not just going in, but also coming out. The danger isn't only in the accumulation period, but it's also in the moment when escape becomes visible and your discipline softens before you've crossed the finish line.

I updated the payment tracker obsessively that final year. Every payment was logged. Every balance recalculated. I of course had a spreadsheet that showed the projected payoff date down to the week. Sometimes down to the day, depending on whether we could squeeze in extra payments here and there.

My wife would sometimes ask, "What's the new date?"

I'd tell her. "Early November, maybe sooner if we can add an extra $500 this month."

She'd nod. She trusted the process, but she also knew better than to ask how many times I'd checked the balance that day. The warrior was still running those numbers even though the keeper was starting to take shape. Sometimes now I think she just asked me about the date to remind me that I didn't need to be in the spreadsheet all the time and that I could also trust the process..

By August, we were under $10,000 in total debt. That threshold felt symbolic. We started at over $107,000. Now we were in four figures. For the first time in years, in decades, really, the debt felt conquerable. We could have drained the modest savings we had built by then or pulled from other accounts and eliminated it right then, but we didn't. The plan was the plan, and we'd committed to paying it down systematically, building emergency savings alongside it, not sacrificing one for the other.

That discipline mattered. It would have felt like cheating to shortcut it at the end, like we'd learned nothing from the process. By October, we were under $5,000. I remember looking at that balance and feeling something unexpected; disoriented. Not relief, not triumph, just disoriented. I hadn't planned beyond that point.

This debt had been part of my life for so long that eliminating it felt like losing something, even though what we were losing was objectively terrible. The vigilance, the identity, the constant monitoring, the budget anxiety, and how we lived our daily lives. Those things had shaped my rhythm for years. Without them, who would I be? What would I do with all that mental space?

Prisoners often experience fear of freedom just before and for a while after being released from custody. They become so conditioned to a controlled environment and routine that the idea of independence causes fear. I was experiencing something similar where I had been controlled by my schedule and obligations for so long that I wasn't sure how to manage the freedom without it.

That's when I realized the post-poverty and post-debt identity crisis wasn't just theory. It was real, and it was happening to me in real-time. The crisis wasn't financial anymore. It was existential.

For years, I knew exactly who I was. I was the person who managed the budget. Who tracked every dollar. Who worked multiple jobs to keep the system running. Who stayed vigilant because relaxing wasn't an option. That identity had been exhausting, but it had also been clear. I knew my role, and I knew what was required of me.

Now the debt was gone. The spreadsheet still existed, but it didn't carry the same weight. The budget still mattered, but it didn't dominate my thoughts the way it once had. And without that constant pressure, without that clear enemy to fight against, I didn't know who I was supposed to be.

The warrior had purpose. Survive. Provide. Protect. Endure. Push through. Keep going no matter what. Those imperatives had shaped every decision I made for decades. They governed how I spent my time, how I spent my energy, and how I spent my money. They had determined what I said yes to and what I said no to. They had defined me.

But what defines the keeper? What does the keeper do when there's no immediate crisis to manage?

I didn't have good answers to those questions. I had to learn them slowly, through trial and error, through watching myself react to situations that no longer required a warrior's response and asking myself, why am I doing this?

The hardest part wasn't the practical adjustments. It wasn't learning to spend money without guilt or tracking the budget less obsessively. Those were behaviors, and behaviors can be changed with practice and intention.

The hardest part was the loss of identity clarity.

I had been a warrior for so long that I didn't know how to be anything else. I didn't know what a non-warrior version of myself looked like. I didn't know what I valued when survival wasn't the primary value. I didn't know what I wanted when "getting through this" was no longer the goal.

That uncertainty was frightening in a way the debt never was.

The debt was scary, but it was also concrete. I could see it. I could measure it. I could fight it. I could track progress against it. The identity crisis was none of those things. It was vague and formless and internal. It didn't show up on a spreadsheet. It couldn't be solved with a budget. It required something the warrior had never developed, introspection without immediate action. The ability to sit with a thought but not respond to it.

My wife noticed before I did. She would ask me what I wanted to do on a free Saturday, and I would freeze. Not because there weren't options, but because I genuinely didn't know. I had spent so many years doing what needed to be done that I had lost touch with what I wanted to do.

I enjoyed things in theory, like hiking, playing guitar, reading for pleasure instead of self-improvement, but I hadn't done them in so long that I wasn't sure they still fit. I had become a person defined entirely by necessity. Without necessity driving me, I didn't know how to move.

The warrior knows how to fight. The keeper has to learn how to live.

That learning process was uncomfortable. It still is. There are days when I slip back into warrior mode because it's familiar and I know how to operate there. The keeper requires something more difficult, something unfamiliar in the system. Trust. It meant trusting that the systems will hold without constant monitoring. Trusting that rest isn't the same as laziness. Trusting that "enough" is safe.

The post-debt identity crisis isn't something most financial books talk about. They focus on getting out of debt, as if elimination is the finish line. But elimination is just the beginning of a different, more complex challenge, like figuring out who you are when you're no longer defined by what you're fighting against.

I'm still working on that. Still learning who the keeper is. Still discovering what I value beyond survival. Still building an identity that isn't shaped entirely by scarcity.

The warrior kept me alive, and I honor that, but the keeper has to teach me how to live, and that's harder work than I expected.

The truck became an unexpected measure of my transition from warrior to keeper.

When I bought it nine days before the layoff, I immediately went into defense mode. Whatever it took, I was going to keep that truck. It wasn't just transportation anymore, it was proof that the layoff hadn't defeated me, that I could still have nice things, and that I hadn't failed.

But somewhere in those first few months, something shifted. Once we realized the severance overlap would work, once the teaching salary proved sustainable, I stopped defending the truck. I just... drove it.

The warrior needs to defend every decision. The keeper doesn't need to defend anything and chooses intentionality.

I still drive that truck today and I love it. But now it's just transportation I chose to keep, not a battle I had to win. That difference, between defending and choosing, is everything.

One evening in late October, she asked, "Are you okay? You seem...off."

I tried to explain that I was excited about reaching the payoff goal. That I knew this was good, but also that I felt strangely unmoored. Like I was about to step off a treadmill I'd been running on for so long I'd forgotten what it felt like to stand still.

I think she understood. She'd been on the treadmill too, though maybe not as intensely. "It's okay to feel weird about it," she said, "We've been fighting this for a long time. It's okay if finishing feels complicated."

That permission helped. It gave me space to feel what I was feeling without forcing myself to move past it. The warrior would have pushed through the discomfort, but the keeper could sit with it.

The final payment was scheduled for November 6th. I had known that date for months. I'd circled it on the calendar. I'd marked it in the spreadsheet. It had taken on almost ceremonial weight in my mind.

But when the day finally came, it was quieter than I expected.

When the final payment was ready to be made, I asked my wife if she wanted to press the button. She did. It was a quick, sort of fly-by moment. She knew I was in the process of making the final payments, and on a whim, I brought the laptop to her after setting up the payment and asked if she wanted to hit "submit" to make our final payment. There was a quick "woohoo!" and then we went about our day. I don't mean to downplay it, but we had been talking about it and preparing for so long it was just like we wanted to get it done and move on.

The Aftermath

The days and weeks following that final payment were surreal in ways I hadn't anticipated.

The balances were zero. Fully zero. I kept opening the credit card apps anyway, checking and rechecking, half-expecting something to materialize. A forgotten subscription or residual interest. Maybe some charge we'd missed or forgotten about. Some lingering ghost from the past that would pull us back in.

I did this multiple times a day for the first week. Morning, lunch, evening, and before bed. Just opening the apps, staring at the zero balances, closing them, then opening them again an hour later as if something might have changed.

My wife caught me doing this one evening. "Still zero?" she asked, gently, but with a touch of deadpan delivery.

"Still zero," I said with a grin.

"You can stop checking now."

"I know."

But I didn't stop. Not yet. The vigilance had been my companion for too long. It didn't disappear just because the threat did.

What slowly started to change was the budget itself. For years, the budget had been dominated by those large debt payments. Now that entire section of the spreadsheet was just...gone. Blank. Irrelevant. In its place were numbers I wasn't used to seeing. There was margin created by surplus. Money that didn't have a job yet because all the old jobs had been eliminated. Finding freedom in the elimination of jobs was not lost on me. I think we all should pay attention when life speaks to us in metaphors.

The first month after payoff, I stared at that surplus line in the budget and felt uncomfortable. This much money just sitting there felt wrong, almost irresponsible. The warrior whispered, "You should be doing something about this. Optimize it. Put it to work. Make it productive."

But the keeper was learning to sit with stillness, with space that didn't require motion. To trust the idea that not every

dollar needed an immediate assignment.
That would come, but not right now.

By the second week, I felt something else
shift. Not relief, exactly, more like...security.
Comfort. The feeling that I could finally
keep my eyes forward instead of constantly
looking over my shoulder to see if my past
was still right on my heels. I knew, finally,
that it wasn't.

Around the third week, I made a decision
that would have been impossible before. I
moved nearly everything to autopay.

Utilities, insurance, phone bill, streaming
subscriptions, basically anything that had a
predictable monthly payment got
automated. No more manual checking. No
more logging into each account to verify the
payment went through. No more hovering
over the submit button wondering if the
money would actually be there.

I did all this in a single day. I went through
the budget line by line and set up autopay
for everything that qualified. The action
itself was sudden, almost impulsive, but the
feeling that allowed it had been building for
several weeks. The trust that the money
would be there. That the system would hold.
That I didn't need to monitor every
transaction to prevent disaster.

That shift represented something more than convenience. For the first time in my adult life, I was trusting systems instead of substituting vigilance for security.

It took a few more weeks before that trust fully settled in. I still checked the accounts more often than necessary. Still reviewed transactions daily even though nothing required my attention. But gradually, the compulsion eased. Days would pass without me opening the banking app. Then a week. Then longer.

The keeper was learning what the warrior never could, that safety doesn't come from constant monitoring, it comes from having enough margin that normal life doesn't register as threat.

Losing Track of Days

Something else shifted during school breaks that would have been unthinkable before. I started losing track of what day of the week it was.

Not in a disoriented or unhealthy way, but in a way that revealed just how completely my relationship with time had changed.

During winter break or summer breaks, I'd wake up and genuinely not know if it was Tuesday or Thursday. The days blurred together, not from exhaustion or dissociation, but from genuine rest and freedom from urgency.

The warrior always knew exactly what day it was. The schedule dictated every moment. Monday meant certain obligations, while Friday meant others, and every day in between had their own commitments. The week was a rigid structure that couldn't be ignored or forgotten because survival depended on knowing where you were in the cycle at all times.

But during breaks, when no classes needed teaching and no immediate deadlines loomed, the days could just...be. I didn't need to know it was Wednesday because Wednesday didn't carry any different weight than Tuesday or Thursday. Time became fluid rather than segmented.

This wasn't irresponsibility. The important things were still handled, but the constant awareness of calendar position, the mental ticker that had run for decades tracking exactly where I was in the week could finally quiet down.

The keeper had created enough margin that during rest periods, time didn't need to be monitored. It could just pass unmarked, unmanaged, and unmonetized. That might seem like a small thing, but it represented a profound shift in how my nervous system was learning to exist in the world.

The Music Shift

Even my relationship with music changed, though it took me a while to notice. Music has always been very important to me. It's rare that I don't have music playing during the day, whether I'm working in my office, making food in the kitchen, or doing something in the garage. I have a portable Bluetooth speaker that generally goes where I go.

I'd grown up with hard rock and heavy metal and have loved it my entire life. The intensity, the speed, the controlled chaos of it. KISS, Black Sabbath, Metallica. Iron Maiden. That music had been the soundtrack of my life for decades. But a few months after the debt was gone, I found myself skipping songs. Reaching for something else. The frenetic energy that had always energized me suddenly felt...wrong. Irritating. Not bad, just mismatched to where I was internally.

I discovered a genre called dark academia, which is piano-centric, sometimes with some cello. It was much slower and more grounding. Contemplative music that asked you to sit with it, not push through it. I also found Viking-themed music that felt strong but not rushed. Deliberate and powerful without being aggressive.

The warrior needed the intense music that matched the internal state of constant motion, constant vigilance, constant fight. Music that drove forward momentum even when my body was exhausted.

The keeper could breathe slower. Could sit with stillness. Could choose music that invited presence instead of demanding performance.

I still love metal. I still listen to it occasionally, but it's no longer my default preference, and that small shift that was barely noticeable on the surface reflected something much deeper about who I was becoming.

Your nervous system speaks in ways you don't always hear consciously. Sometimes it speaks through what music feels right. Through what pace your body wants to move at. Whether stillness feels comfortable or threatening. Mine was learning, slowly, to prefer the stillness.

Food and the Keeper's Relationship with Enough

Eventually my relationship with food changed, and like the music shift, I didn't notice it immediately.

Growing up poor, you learn to clean your plate. Food waste equals money waste. You eat what's in front of you, whether you're hungry or not, because the opportunity might not come again soon. That pattern followed me into adulthood, long after scarcity was the reality.

For years I regularly ate past fullness. Not out of enjoyment, but out of obligation. The plate was there. The food was there. Throwing it away felt wrong, wasteful, and irresponsible. So, I finished it, even when my body was signaling it had enough.

After the debt was gone and margin became real, something shifted. I started choosing smaller portions. Not to save money, though that was a welcome side effect, but because I could finally hear what my body was trying to tell me about hunger and fullness.

I also started prioritizing food quality over simple cost. For years, every food decision ran through the budget filter first. What's cheapest? What's on sale? What stretches furthest? Quality was a luxury that came after survival.

The keeper could ask different questions. What will better nourish me? What do I want to eat, not just what can I afford? What portion size matches my actual hunger?

This wasn't about health fads or diet culture. It was about listening instead of overriding. About choosing intentionally instead of just consuming functionally. About recognizing that enough food on my plate looked different than it did when scarcity shaped every meal.

The warrior ate everything because waste was inexcusable. The keeper ate until he was satisfied, and that was enough.

Learning to Navigate Margin

We had gone from just over $107,000 in revolving credit card debt that went from being feared to being managed to being normalized, and then finally to zero balances across the board. There was also a quiet belief that this time would be different. That's why structure was still so important. Structure was crucial to success then, more than ever.

Our debt payoff happened right before Christmas. The temptation was immediate. After years of discipline, after finally clearing the balances, we were very tempted to go overboard. To celebrate. To reward ourselves. To buy freely for the first time without the hangover that follows.

Thankfully, we didn't do that. We avoided the entitlement trap, and we stuck to the agreement that we would only spend what we had planned and saved for. Nothing more. The temptation wasn't to be extravagant; it was to be generous. Giving our kids and family the kind of holiday we hadn't been able to afford before. There wasn't much else we wanted.

We typically budgeted to give the kids a nice Christmas in terms of gifts, but we had an urge to go above. We decided against our urges because it wouldn't align with our plan, our budget, or ability to give as heavily next year. We chose consistency in order to keep the new foundation we were building intact.

There is a temptation, once margin appears, to become generous too quickly. To your kids, to family, to strangers, to causes that speak directly to the parts of you that remember how hard things once were. Your heart grows faster than your systems stabilize. Lottery winners fall into this trap all the time. So do people who finally escape scarcity. Generosity is a beautiful instinct, but if it's reactive instead of intentional, it becomes another form of self-erasure. Margins must be built and protected before they can be shared.

What kept us from backsliding wasn't motion. It was a new type of vigilance. Not hyper-vigilance, but purposeful vigilance. The wounds of debt were fresh and real, and we were very ready for healing. We were ready to build something foundational; something generational. Once the realization of a comfortable retirement hit us, once we understood what $3,200 a month in freed-up cash flow could do if invested instead of being paid out to past credit card obligations, we were more committed than ever to make that reality happen. We were also aware of the temptation that much new cash flow brought. This danger zone is very real.

The Christmas discipline was important, but it was also easy in some ways. Christmas was a single, contained event. We knew it was coming. We'd prepared for it. We made a conscious decision and stuck to it.

The harder temptations were the small, unplanned ones. The ones that snuck up during ordinary moments throughout the day.

We'd go to the store for a few small things, like milk or bread, or some other necessities, and suddenly the cart would be full. Not with extravagant purchases, just...things. A new kitchen gadget that seemed useful. A few extra items that were on sale. Some organizational bins we didn't really need but might use someday.

None of them were individually significant but added together it represented something dangerous. The slow erosion of discipline and the gradual drift back toward using money without intention.

One day, maybe two months after debt payoff, we were at Target for a few small household necessities. We left with $150 worth of stuff. Not because we needed it, but because we could afford it. Because the cushion was there. Because saying yes felt better than saying no.

On the way to car, I looked at my wife and said, "We just did it again."

She knew exactly what I meant. We talked about this pattern. We had recognized it, named it, and still fell into it.

"We have to stop doing this," I said.

"I know."

The realization hit both of us at the same time The margin we'd fought so hard to create could be destroyed just as easily as we'd built it. Not through catastrophe, but through carelessness. Through the accumulation of small yeses that should have been nos. Through immediate gratification that should have been planned. Death by a thousand cuts.

Our actions going forward would either grow and protect our margin or destroy it. This was entirely about behavior now, not about math. The math was fine, and it would stay fine for as long as our behavior supported it.

We implemented some new rules after that. If we saw something we wanted, we could add it to a list. If we still wanted it the next time we went shopping, and if it fit the budget, we could buy it. We also budgeted some personal allowance we would keep in our own accounts that didn't require planning or discussion, but impulse was no longer allowed to drive the decisions for our household.

That simple rule saved us countless times over the following months. The planning buffer created space between want and action. Most of the time, the want faded. Occasionally it didn't, and we'd buy the thing, but deliberately, not reactively.

This danger zone wasn't behind us. It was right here, in the space between discipline and abundance. In the gap between having margin and protecting it. That's where post-debt crisis lives. Not in the elimination of debt, but in the months after, when the old guardrails are gone and the new ones haven't been fully internalized yet. This is when the new identity is growing but has not fully developed. It isn't yet in control of daily behavior.

Budgeting didn't disappear when the pressure eased, it evolved. It stopped requiring hypervigilance and became reliable. The system still existed, but it no longer needed micromanagement. Volatility gave way to predictability. Money shifted from being a symbol of fear to something that could be used deliberately, but carefully and with intention.

One of the first moments I noticed this change surprised me with its simplicity. After a heavy snowstorm, I decided to pay someone to clear our driveway. For most of my life, that would have been unthinkable. Snow removal was something I did myself, no matter the cold, no matter the pain in my back, no matter the time. Paying someone else felt indulgent, even lazy. I had paid for snow removal only once before, years earlier. It was uncomfortable then and I only did it then because it was a family trying to raise some money, and I wanted to help them. Even that act of support felt like indulgence, like I was paying for something I should have been doing myself. This time, however, it felt perfectly fine. Reasonable, even.

I stood at the window drinking a cup of coffee, just watching and feeling the moment. The gratitude was very sobering in the sense that it was a step, however small, forward in my behavior, not just the math. I was doing something different. It was here; it was now.

There were other moments too. We bought
a brand-new dining room table and chairs
set, and some home decor. Small things, but
things that had been put off for a long time
because they were either not possible or not
a priority against everything else. My wife
felt the shift as much as I did. We didn't
have to point it out to each other. We both
knew. This wasn't waste, this was margin
being used appropriately, and that changed
how we saw everything.

We had walked through Ikea during a
birthday trip to St. Louis for my wife. We
looked at tables there and decided to put
one on our short list of improvements we
were budgeting for. We deliberately avoided
buying one while we were there, which
would have been easier, but wouldn't have
been planned or budgeted for. We also went
and looked at a used set the next week that
was for sale on the community social media
page. We took the cash, fully intending to
buy it if we liked it. It was ok, not exactly
what we wanted, and needed a bit of repair.
It would have been something we probably
would have bought in the past. A temporary
patch. Good enough for now. But that day
we left without it. When we got home, I
started browsing online for new ones and
we decided we were going to buy a new one.
We could afford it now, and we kind of felt
like we deserved it at this point. We didn't

go overboard, and we didn't buy on impulse. We planned for it and bought a reasonable set, appropriate for our space. A month later we were still commenting to each other about how much we love it and just liked looking at it sometimes. That's how unfamiliar a simple piece of new furniture was to us! Looking back, it occurred to me that at 52 years old, this was the very first brand-new full size dining room table and chairs set I ever had. Wow.

That's when I began to understand what enough really meant. Enough wasn't a number, it was stable income without escalation. Enough was time that didn't need to be monetized. Enough was the ability to absorb normal life events without panic. Enough meant no longer requiring perfect conditions just to feel safe. Enough was mental space without agendas.

The concept of "enough" became clear during the process of paying off debt and feeling the relief of having margin.

It all happened gradually. There was no urgency anymore, nothing that needed addressed right away, and if it did, we could handle it without much interruption. My days now, all of them, had time that was discretionary. I could decide how to fill that time. I had boundaries that protected my availability. I finally felt like I was able to let go of some things, and at that moment, the idea of having enough settled over me.

You can do a lot more with modest income and wide margin than you can with high income and narrow margin. Not just financially, but in all areas of life. That realization didn't arrive all at once either. It settled in gradually as the pressure eased. There wasn't a specific conversation where my wife and I acknowledged "we're okay now", we just felt it. The tone of our conversations shifted. The future we wanted and talked about in vague, distant terms was finally a reality. Retirement moved from "someday, maybe" to "realistic and achievable".

When Someday Became Real

The shift in our retirement planning was possibly the fastest and most powerful change after debt elimination.

For years, retirement had been an abstract thought; a vague "someday" that existed in theory but not in practice. We contributed to retirement accounts, but only enough to get any available employer match, but not much beyond that. The debt payments consumed too much cash flow to allow anything more than barely modest retirement saving. That's a very real and painful example of opportunity cost.

We knew intellectually that we were behind. That we'd need to catch up eventually, but "eventually" always felt distant. Something to worry about later when the debt was gone and margin existed.

Now "later" was here, and with it came a jarring realization that we weren't just behind, we were significantly behind. If we wanted to retire comfortably in our mid-60s, we had about 15 years to build what we should have already been building for the past 25 years or longer.

That would have felt crushing before, but now it felt possible.

The $3,200 that had been going to debt payments could now go to retirement savings. Not all of it though. We would need to maintain emergency savings, build other reserves, and keep some breathing room in the budget. But even half of that freed-up cash flow, invested consistently, would make an enormous difference over 15 years or so.

I did the calculations obsessively in those first few months with different contribution amounts, different portfolio allocations, different return assumptions, and different retirement ages. The spreadsheets multiplied as I modeled every scenario I could think of.

But something else happened that I hadn't anticipated. Margins began to grow in other, unexpected ways.

When you're in crisis mode, consumed by debt payments and constant financial vigilance, you don't have bandwidth to optimize anything. You're in survival mode and maintaining but not improving. Once the debt was gone and mental space opened up, I could finally look at other systems that for years largely felt out of my control.

Health insurance was the first domino. With my new employment my wife and I were no longer stuck with the same options for insurance. I spent time analyzing our usage patterns, reviewing the formulary, calculating premiums and out-of-pocket maximums under different scenarios, and comparing the costs and benefits between plans. We switched to a different plan structure that matched our needs and the result was that our annual costs dropped by almost 50%.

Then car and home insurance were next. Same story. We'd been with the same provider for years. We had adequate coverage, predictable payments, and no reason to change when every hour was already spoken for. But finally, I had time to get competitive quotes, review coverage details, and understand what we truly needed versus what we'd been carrying out of inertia. We consolidated both policies with a different provider and ended up with better coverage at a lower cost, about 37% reduction in annual premiums.

These weren't windfalls. They were optimization opportunities that had always existed, I just never had the bandwidth to pursue them when every ounce of mental energy was dedicated to debt management and survival.

Then other unexpected changes started appearing. I received a two percent raise after just six months with the university, which was modest, but meaningful. My wife transferred into a new role with less stress and higher pay. These weren't things we'd orchestrated or fought for, they just...happened, as if the universe recognized we'd finally created space and decided to fill it with blessings.

Added together, these changes freed up several thousand dollars annually. More money that could flow directly into retirement savings and money that widened our margin even further and provided capacity we didn't think possible.

This is what I hadn't understood about margin before, it compounds. Not just financially, but systematically. When you're not in survival mode, you can see opportunities you were blind to before. You can make changes that create more space, which creates more capacity, which creates more opportunities. The cycle runs in reverse, not in a downward spiral, but an upward one.

I've taught countless finance, economics, and accounting classes with many lessons about compounding but never thought of it in this context until I went through it for myself. Now I have another life lesson to pass on to my students that fits within conceptual framework of their studies.

The warrior had fought to create margin through sheer force. The keeper was learning that once margin exists, it tends to grow on its own if you protect it and pay attention.

What struck me most wasn't the numbers themselves, though they were encouraging, but what the numbers represented. For the first time in my life, retirement wasn't a wish. It was a plan. Not "I hope we can retire someday", but "We will retire, and here's when and how."

That shift from an abstract hope to a concrete timeline changed everything. It turned "I wish" into "I will." It made the future feel closer, more tangible, and more real. This revealed a long-held assumption that I carried under the surface. That I would always work, even into retirement. Not for enjoyment, but out of necessity. That was something I just assumed would be part of my life and had never considered an alternative. It was a startling realization that I no longer had to plan on that. That I could truly retire completely, or if I still wanted to work in some capacity, it would be completely voluntary and for my own enjoyment. This meant more options, better options.

But it also did something else unexpected. It slowed down my perception of time.

When you're drowning in debt, time moves differently. Every day is urgent, every week is a sprint. You're always racing toward the next payment, the next crisis, or the next thing that needs managing. Time collapses into a narrow present tense, and when I say tense, I mean that as both how it relates to time and also a reflection of your physical and mental state.

When margin exists and the future becomes plannable, time expands. You can think in years, not weeks. You can make decisions that won't pay off for a decade. You can be patient. You can convert that emotional urgency into a process that carries the weight instead of your mind and spirit. That alone has real and significant mental and physical health improvement outcomes.

The retirement planning conversations my wife and I had were different now. We talked about what we wanted retirement to look like, not just financially, but experientially. Where we might live. How we'd spend our time. What mattered to us. These were concrete, material plans, no longer just dreams.

We talked about travel. Not extravagant trips but visiting our kids who were scattered across the country, seeing our grandchildren grow up, and having the freedom to leave for a week without worrying about income or obligations.

We talked about hobbies I'd set aside for years. Things I used to do when I had time, like foraging for mushrooms, reading for pleasure, not just professional development, and having conversations that didn't need to be productive, they were just interesting. Maybe sitting in a coffee shop slowly enjoying a local roast without the rush of the day pushing me forward.

These weren't fantasies anymore, they were plans. And that difference between a "someday" fantasy and planned future with a timeline marked the completion of something I'd been building toward my entire adult life without fully realizing it.

The warrior had kept me alive long enough to reach this point, but the keeper was learning to protect what the warrior had built, and somewhere, quietly, the sage was beginning to emerge, not yet fully formed, but present enough to recognize that significance isn't measured in what you accumulate, it's measured in what you make possible for yourself, for the people you love, and for those who come after.

The calculation was simple. Having gone from $3,200 in monthly debt payments to $0, it meant much of that new surplus was now available for retirement investment. Even though we had a shorter runway than if we'd started years earlier, we could now invest aggressively. The sacrifice ahead would be real and more concentrated than it would have been if we had started earlier, but it was voluntary now and the timeline was clear. Voluntary sacrifice feels entirely different than involuntary sacrifice, and now it is no longer tied to endurance, it's the result of intention.

I was still constantly doing the calculations. It's not that we never invested in our retirement, it's just that we were so constrained by all the other financial obligations that it was insufficient for a comfortable retirement, or even a full retirement. But now, those constraints are gone and we could significantly boost our contributions. I won't give the exact numbers, but it's enough that we will be able to retire on our terms.

What we were doing now still looked like sacrifice, but it felt different. This is where the identity shift happens. The warrior survives through endurance. The keeper protects through restraint. The warrior asks, how much more can I carry? The keeper asks, what no longer needs to be carried at all? The warrior's sacrifice is involuntary; the keeper's sacrifice is voluntary; and the sage's sacrifice becomes legacy.

Keeper behavior looks different in practice. It's being intentionally slow with your daily pace. Taking time for regular walks, not just functional exercise, but movement for its own sake. Making meals instead of grabbing what's fast and convenient. It's sitting at peace, without the need to fill every moment with productivity. Making time, not finding time.

These may seem like small things, but they represent a fundamental shift. Knowing when enough is truly enough is still an ongoing practice for me. It hasn't become fully natural yet. Decades of perspective and behavior aren't undone overnight, or even in a few months. I still catch myself monitoring, calculating, scanning for risk even when there's no risk present. The guilt has mostly faded, though. Some things, some purchases, some moments of free time still feel awkward at times. Unfamiliar, like wearing clothes that fit but aren't broken-in yet.

That discomfort is part of the transition. The warrior kept me alive, but living and surviving are not the same thing, and slowly, I'm learning the difference.

I eventually realized that money was never the point, margin was, and margin shows up everywhere, not just in bank accounts. You cannot spreadsheet your way out of a nervous system shaped by scarcity and hyper-vigilance, but you can build a life that no longer demands it.

This chapter isn't about winning, it's about stopping. Knowing when effort has done its job. Knowing when motion is no longer protective. Knowing when enough is truly enough and learning to live there without guilt. It's about living with hard-earned peace and allowing yourself to accept it.

Chapter 10: The Three Identities Framework

The shift from one way of living to another doesn't announce itself clearly. There's no ceremony, no moment when you consciously decide to become someone different. What happens instead is gradual; a slow recognition that the strategies that once kept you alive are now keeping you from growing in many ways.

Throughout this book, I've described my journey through three distinct identities, the warrior, the keeper, and the sage. These aren't arbitrary labels; they're patterns I recognized only after I had the distance and space to look back and name what had been happening all along.

The warrior identity doesn't respect boundaries between life domains. You might think you've left warrior mode at work, but find it running your parenting, your health, your friendships, or your rest. The keeper has to recognize where the warrior is still operating, not to eliminate it everywhere at once, but to analyze its engagement and ask, is this identity still serving me here?

Warrior with health looks like ignoring pain signals, working through illness, treating your body like a machine that must perform regardless of what it's telling you. It sounds like "I don't have time to be sick" or "I'll rest when this project is done" or "Pain is just weakness leaving the body." The warrior doesn't listen to the body, it overrides it. Every symptom becomes an obstacle to push through rather than information to consider. Health becomes an inconvenience rather than a priority.

Warrior with relationships looks like never saying no, over-committing to everyone, and sacrificing presence for productivity. It's being physically present but mentally elsewhere. It's helping everyone else while your own needs go unmet. The warrior believes love is measured by how much you can carry for others, so boundaries feel like failure.

Warrior with rest looks like guilt when you're not working, the inability to relax without having "earned it" first, treating vacation as an interruption. It's the voice that says, "other people are getting ahead while you're just sitting here" or "you should be doing something productive, and rest isn't productive." The warrior can only rest when forced by illness, injury, or exhaustion, and even then, it feels like losing ground. Leisure isn't rejuvenating, it's anxiety-inducing.

Warrior with emotions looks like "push through", "don't be weak", "I don't have time to process this right now". Feelings become distractions from the mission. Grief is scheduled for later and anxiety gets ignored until it turns into panic. Joy feels uncomfortable because it requires letting your guard down. The warrior treats emotional processing the same way it treats physical pain, as something to power through rather than attend to.

You might be a keeper with your money, budgeting thoughtfully, building margin, making intentional choices, while still operating as a warrior with your body, relationships, and rest. These identities can coexist in different areas of your life. Recognizing where each one is active is the first step toward deciding whether that's still serving you.

The warrior is forged in scarcity, the keeper emerges with recognition, and the sage develops in abundance. Not material abundance necessarily, but abundance of margins, wisdom, and peace. Let's be honest though, if you reach this point, it is likely to appear to others as material abundance, although that's not the goal itself.

Most people spend their entire lives in warrior mode without ever recognizing it. They believe they're simply being responsible, diligent, hardworking, which are all true, but they're also bleeding for ghosts. They're expending energy on threats that no longer exist, carrying armor they no longer need, and fighting battles that ended years ago.

Understanding these identities isn't about self-improvement. It's about self-awareness. It's about recognizing which identity is driving your decisions right now, and whether that identity still serves you.

The Warrior Identity

The warrior develops when margin doesn't exist. When every decision carries weight it shouldn't have to carry. When surprises become threats and rest feels dangerous.

When I use the word "warrior", I'm not talking about someone clad in armor charging into battle, and I'm not romanticizing struggle or celebrating exhaustion as virtue.

I'm talking about someone whose nervous system has been trained by scarcity to stay perpetually alert. Someone who survives through endurance because circumstances haven't allowed any other option. Someone who equates motion with safety, rest with danger, and vigilance with responsibility.

The warrior is the identity that forms when threats, whether real or perceived, are constant. It's the posture your body and mind adopt when the environment demands relentless effort just to keep systems from collapsing.

This isn't strength for strength's sake. It's survival adaptation, and it works until it doesn't. It's when the threats recede but the vigilance remains. It's when you're safe but still can't rest. It's after you've built margin but can't access it because the warrior won't let go.

That's the warrior I'm describing. Not a hero, not an ideal, just a pattern of being that kept you alive when nothing else would have but holds you back when those behaviors are no longer necessary.

You become a warrior not through choice but through necessity. The environment demands it. Scarcity trains your nervous system to stay alert, to anticipate, to never fully relax. Problems aren't solved, only managed. Stability isn't achieved; it's maintained through constant vigilance.

The warrior learns that:

· Exhaustion equals responsibility

· Rest must be earned, never freely taken

· Asking for help is a last resort

· Motion equals safety

· Stopping, even briefly, invites danger

These beliefs aren't taught explicitly, they're absorbed. They become the operating system running beneath everything else. They're quietly shaped over years of environmental conditioning.

The warrior is extraordinary at survival, at holding systems together under pressure, and at making things work with whatever resources are available. The warrior can endure conditions that would break others.

But the warrior cannot rest. Cannot delegate. Cannot trust that things will hold together without constant monitoring. The warrior confuses vigilance with safety, motion with progress, and exhaustion with virtue.

I was in warrior mode for over thirty years. That identity kept me alive. It helped me escape poverty, build a career, support a family, and shoulder responsibilities that often felt heavier than I was ready for. The warrior succeeded at exactly what it was designed to do.

The problem wasn't that the warrior failed. The problem was that the warrior didn't know when to stop.

The Keeper Identity

The keeper doesn't arrive dramatically. There's no single moment when you decide to stop being a warrior. The biggest hurdle is that the keeper doesn't always make itself known. Recognizing the keeper requires time and space for reflection, neither of which you may have at the moment. You may live for many years, as I did, with an unnecessary warrior identity before recognizing the keeper is what you need now. This above anything else is what I hope I can deliver to you in this book. The ability to recognize your identity in this regard.

The keeper appears when you are able to recognize:

· The immediate threats have receded

· Some financial breathing room is possible

· Time doesn't need to be completely consumed by crisis management

· You have enough space to ask, "What do I actually want to protect?"

These changes may not be obvious to you at all. You may even want to deny they exist for a while because you're afraid to let your guard down. "What if..." keeps us vigilant.

Keeper doesn't develop quickly, even after recognition. If the warrior was able to develop and operate for over 30 years, the

keeper may take years too. You owe it to
yourself to allow plenty of grace to let this
evolve.

Early Keeper

The early keeper still means fighting warrior
impulses daily. Guilt surfaces when you rest.
Anxiety appears when you're not
monitoring. You're learning to trust systems
without constant checking, but the trust
doesn't come naturally yet. You make
mistakes, like slipping back into warrior
mode during stress or overcorrecting into
paralysis where you can't make any decision
at all. The early keeper feels uncomfortable,
unfamiliar, and sometimes wrong. The
warrior's voice is loud, questioning every
choice, "Are you sure this is safe? Shouldn't
you be doing more?"

Mid Keeper

The mid keeper means the foundation is
solid and boundaries mostly hold. The
warrior still returns occasionally, and that's
okay. You can recognize it faster now and
respond with intention instead of just
reacting. Building margin becomes more
natural, less forced. Saying no doesn't
require the same internal battle it once did.
The mid keeper starts feeling more like
returning home than being in a war zone.
You're not fighting to maintain it every day;

you're living it most days with occasional
warrior interruptions. You may even
recognize times when it's appropriate to let
the warrior return, but with purpose. That's
a real characteristic of the keeper, living
with intention, not reaction.

Mature Keeper

The mature keeper is when the identity has
become a default setting, not a daily
decision. The warrior returns only by
invitation, and for genuine crises, not
manufactured ones. Margins are protected
instinctively, without constant deliberation.
This is where glimpses of the sage identity
start emerging naturally. The keeper
identity has depth now, history, roots. It's
not something you're simply trying to
become; it's something you are, that will be
tested over many years and seasons.

The timeline depends on how deep your
warrior identity ran, how long you operated
in survival mode, and how much support
you have in the transition. Someone who
was a warrior for five years will likely
transition faster than someone who was a
warrior for thirty. Don't rush it and don't
compare your timeline to anyone else's. The
keeper can't be forced, only cultivated.

This shift is harder than it sounds. The
warrior's strategies are deeply embedded.

Your nervous system doesn't update automatically just because circumstances improve. You've spent years, maybe decades, training yourself to scan for threats, to stay perpetually ready, and to never fully exhale.

The keeper must learn to:

· Trust systems instead of constantly monitoring them

· Set boundaries around time, energy, and availability

· Distinguish between productivity and presence

· Practice restraint instead of accumulation

· Recognize when "enough" is truly enough

The keeper's primary work isn't building more; it's protecting what matters. This includes protecting yourself, your health, your relationships, your peace, and your capacity to think clearly.

In practical terms, keeper behavior looks like:

· Moving payments to autopay instead of manually checking every transaction

· Recognizing when something isn't urgent, like allowing receipts to accumulate for a few days rather than updating the budget immediately

· Paying someone to clear snow instead of doing it yourself despite physical pain

· Saying no to opportunities that would generate income but erode margin

· Taking time off without guilt or the need to justify it

· Sitting with your own thoughts and embracing the quiet

· Thoughtful presence with loved ones that doesn't look or feel transactional

These actions might seem small, but they represent a fundamental identity shift. The warrior may see them as weakness or waste, but the keeper sees them as healthy and necessary, and the inevitable foundation for the sage's wisdom.

The danger zone for the keeper isn't crisis, it's complacency. Once the pressure lifts and credit cards sit empty, it's easy to slip back into old patterns. Not through dramatic failure, but through gradual erosion. Small justifications. One purchase that "doesn't matter". One boundary that "isn't a big deal". One month where you don't quite follow through.

The keeper must remain intentional without becoming hypervigilant. This is the balance that takes time to learn. Creating clear boundaries helps to automate the intention.

Write them, say them. Confide in someone you trust with what you're going through, or if you're married or have a partner, be transparent with them and accept their support.

My transition from warrior to keeper took a little over two years, and I'm still in the process. I would say as I write this, I'm probably still in early keeper identity, but almost to mid keeper. Although the debt was eliminated in less time, the posture remained several months afterward. I reviewed and updated the budget several times a week, even when there was no threat. I kept myself tethered online "just in case" long after there was no system that needed my attention. I kept bracing for impact even when nothing was coming.

The keeper isn't weak, however, the keeper just knows how and when to be strong. The keeper is deliberate, and deliberate action, after decades of reactive motion, feels uncomfortably slow at first.

The Sage Identity

I haven't arrived here yet. I'm writing about the sage identity from observation and aspiration rather than complete embodiment. That honesty matters because the sage isn't a finish line you cross, it's a way of being that develops over years, maybe decades, of living as a keeper. In many ways it's the culmination of the outcomes you experience as a result of the keeper's intentionality, boundaries, and purposeful movement since letting the tired warrior rest.

The sage emerges when the keeper's work has become second nature. When margins aren't something you're still fighting to build or protect, they simply exist naturally and permanently. When intentionality no longer requires constant attention because it's been internalized as your default way of moving through the world.

Where the warrior survives and the keeper protects, the sage contributes. Not from obligation or guilt, but from overflow. From a place of genuine abundance that shows up as abundance of time, wisdom, peace, and resources that aren't tied to your own survival needs. When you've accepted that you have more than "enough" you're able to pass the rest along.

The sage's orientation shifts outward:

· From "How do I protect what I have?" to "What can I offer?"

· From guarding boundaries to knowing when boundaries can flex

· From personal stability to generational impact

· From lived experience to transmissible wisdom

This doesn't mean the sage is wealthy in the conventional sense, though by this point financial security likely exists. It means the sage has reached a point where the giving of time, attention, knowledge, or other resources doesn't threaten their own foundation. In fact, the sage finds that, despite our traditional thinking, giving leaves us with more than we started with.

The sage can mentor without an agenda. Can give without obligation. Can be generous without self-erasure. The sage learned what the warrior never knew and the keeper slowly discovered that true security comes not from accumulation but from having enough margin that life's normal disruptions don't register as threats. It is with this quiet confidence that giving can become growth.

I see glimpses of the sage in:

· My teaching, when I'm not performing competence but genuinely investing in students' growth. When I'm teaching outside of the lesson and outside of the classroom.

· Conversations with my wife that aren't about problem-solving but simply about being present with gratitude.

· Advising others on their finances without imposing my own story onto their situation

· The ability to rest freely without obligation

· Moments when I can guide others through a problem without immediately trying to fix it

· Interactions with my kids and grandkids

But I also see how far I have yet to go. The sage lives with calm and ease that I haven't fully achieved yet. The sage doesn't merely tolerate uncertainty, they expect, but they are not intimidated or destabilized by it. The sage has perspective that comes from years of living intentionally, not just surviving skillfully. We would typically call this wisdom, but it's more than that.

The sage work I'm most interested in exploring is generational change. Not just teaching my own children about different patterns around money and work, though that matters, but having broader conversations about how identity shapes financial behavior, how nervous systems trained in scarcity create cycles that persist even when circumstances improve, and how recognition of these patterns can create different outcomes.

This book is part of that work. It's me seeing the horizon of the sage identity, looking back at the warrior I was, embracing the keeper I'm becoming, and trying to offer language and recognition to others who might be somewhere on the same path.

The sage doesn't need to have all the answers. The sage just needs to have walked far enough to turn around and say, "I remember what that felt like. Here's what I've learned. Here's what helped. Here's what you might notice if you pay attention."

What the Sage Knows That Others Don't

The sage understands something fundamental that the keeper is still building; that systems are more powerful than effort, and intention is more valuable than motivation.

The warrior believes that effort conquers all obstacles. Work harder, push further, carry more. The keeper learns that boundaries and intentionality matter more than raw output. This isn't the absence of motion, but the deliberate and calculated use of it. Protecting you from engaging in motion where it's not needed. But the sage recognizes that the most powerful intervention is often the one that changes the system itself, not just how you respond to it.

In practical terms, this means:

The warrior sees a broken process and patches it or works around it, while the

keeper protects themselves from the broken
process, and the sage redesigns the process,
so it doesn't break in the first place.

The warrior learns self-reinforcement
internally through endurance and force,
while the keeper learns externally by the
observation of boundaries, and the sage,
who has teaches what they've already
learned directly by asking questions that
help others discover their own answers.

The warrior earns money through motion
and extraordinary effort, while the keeper
saves money and protects margin through
planning, automation, and intentionality,
and the sage defines wealth for themselves
and then amplifies it through compounding
and strategic generosity.

The sage also understands diminishing
returns in ways the warrior never could. The
warrior believes more is always better, that
more income, more credentials, and more
responsibility move us forward. The keeper
learns that "enough" exists, but the sage
knows exactly where the point of enough
sits for them, and they're not interested in
exceeding it just to prove they can. When
they do find excess in their lives they look
for ways to bless someone else with it.

The Sage's Relationship with Time

Perhaps the most visible difference between identities is how they relate to time.

The warrior is always racing against time. Every moment must be productive. Rest is waste. Stillness is risk. Time is the enemy that's always restricting us.

The keeper begins to reclaim time. To protect it. To recognize that unscheduled time isn't empty time, it's space where thinking, recovery, and connection can happen. The keeper creates an environment for growth.

The sage views time as the ultimate non-renewable resource. The sage has internalized that you cannot save time, you can only spend it. The question is whether you're spending it on what matters.

The sage is comfortable with slowness. With processes that unfold over years, not weeks. With investments that include financial, relational, and developmental resources that won't pay off until long after the work is done. The sage can plant trees they'll never sit under without resentment, because they understand legacy in ways the warrior and keeper don't quite grasp.

Sage is the hardest identity to reach because it requires releasing what the warrior and keeper both protect in their own ways, control, recognition, and certainty of outcome.

Ego is likely the first obstacle. Sage requires releasing the need for recognition. If you find yourself thinking "Will anyone know I did this?" or "Will I get credit for this contribution?" you're not ready for sage work yet, and that's okay. The warrior seeks external recognition to justify their efforts, and the keeper seeks internal validation to maintain boundaries, but the sage gives anonymously, mentors people who may never see succeed, and plants trees knowing they'll never sit in the shade of.

Transactional thinking is the second obstacle. "What's in it for me?" and "What will I get back?" are warrior and keeper questions, which are legitimate questions for those identities, but sage gives without measuring return, and in fact, doesn't expect it at all. This doesn't mean being taken advantage of. It means contribution for the sake of others, teaching students you'll never see again, sharing knowledge that might benefit someone you'll never meet, creating generational change in your family tree. The sage has security through what the keeper built, and now the question becomes what to do with the overflow.

Scarcity mindset is the third obstacle. "If I give this knowledge away, I'll have less" or "Someone might use this against me" are warrior protections. The sage knows that contribution doesn't deplete resources, it multiplies them. Teaching your best insights doesn't diminish them. Sharing what you learned the hard way doesn't make your experience less valuable. The sage open-sources wisdom, not to lose advantage, but because wisdom compounds when it's shared.

Timeline expectations are the final obstacle. The warrior needs to see results now. Immediate gratification. The keeper builds for the future they will personally experience. The sage plants seeds for generations they'll never meet. Benjamin Franklin left $2000 each to Boston and Philadelphia in 1790 with instructions that it had to be invested and couldn't be accessed for 200 years. By 1990, it had grown to $6.5 million. He knew he'd never see the impact. That's sage work that looks like contribution beyond your own timeline.

You can perform sage behaviors before being the sage. You can mentor, give, teach, but performing sage behaviors and being the sage are different. Being the sage means you've released the need for it to benefit you directly. That release may be the most meaningful of all.

This is why the sage can mentor effectively. Mentorship requires patience, but it also requires giving time to support outcomes you can't control and may never witness. It requires trusting that the seed you planted will grow, even if you're not there to see the fruits of your effort.

Generational Change: Breaking Cycles That Span Lifetimes

When I talk about generational change, I'm talking about interrupting patterns that don't just shape one life, they shape families, communities, and entire lineages.

I watched my grandparents work themselves into exhaustion. I watched near-constant motion get absorbed into obligations rather than lead to abundance. I was shaped by their beliefs about money, work, and safety without anyone ever sitting me down to explain them. Those beliefs followed me into adulthood, into my career, into my marriages, and into how I raised my own children.

For years, I thought I was doing something different. I wasn't poor anymore. I had education, professional credentials, and a career trajectory that looked nothing like theirs. But underneath all of that, I was operating from the same nervous system. The same scarcity conditioning. The same belief that rest was dangerous and that safety came from staying ahead through sheer effort.

I was perpetuating the cycle in a different form.

Generational change doesn't mean your children won't struggle, but hopefully they'll struggle with fewer and lighter problems. It means they won't inherit your scarcity posture as their default operating system. It means they will have better tools and language to work through things more effectively and on an appropriate timeline. It means they will live their lives more intentionally and less reactively.

What Generational Change Actually Looks Like

For my own children, generational change looks like:

· Being told explicitly that credit cards were to be avoided, and helping them understand why

· Modeling what it looks like to say no to opportunities that erode family time

· Letting them see me turn down promotions that came with prestige but would have opportunity cost through lost margins

· Teaching them that rest isn't earned, it's required

· Showing them that boundaries aren't selfish, they're necessary

· Being transparent about money without making it a source of anxiety

· Writing this book to show them that vulnerability is key to understanding yourself

But I also made a lot of mistakes. I worked too much during their childhoods. I modeled endurance in ways that probably taught them the wrong lessons about what success requires. I didn't always protect my time with them because I was too busy protecting income and staying in motion.

The sage's work isn't perfection, it's course correction. It's naming the patterns you absorbed and deciding which ones serve you and which ones may harm you and consciously choosing what you'll pass forward.

Beyond Your Own Family

Generational change extends beyond your household. It shows up in how you lead, how you teach, how you advise, and how you show up in your community.

When I teach now, I'm not just teaching course content. I'm teaching students, many of whom are first-generation college students like I was, that exhaustion isn't a virtue. That boundaries matter. That enough is a real assessment, not just something people say.

I watch students absorb the same warrior conditioning I did. They work full-time while carrying full course loads. They're sacrificing sleep, health, relationships. They're doing exactly what I did, and they believe it's the only path forward. For some of them that may be true...for now, but I hope they don't turn a sprint into a marathon like I did.

Part of the sage growth is about showing them a different model. Not by telling them to work less, I can't make that choice for them, and many truly don't have that option right now. But by helping them see the pattern, name it, and recognize when the war is over.

When I advise clients on their finances, I'm not just helping them build retirement portfolios. I'm helping them understand how their relationship with money may be shaped by environments they didn't choose,

and how those patterns affect their
decisions today.

The sage's generational work is about
recognition and language. Giving people the
tools to see what's happening so they can
choose differently, not prescribing answers
but helping others ask better questions.

The Long View

The warrior doesn't have time for the long
view. The horizon is always right in front of
them, in the form of the next paycheck, the
next crisis, or the next urgent obligation.

The keeper begins to extend the horizon
with things like retirement planning,
children's futures, and the shape of the next
five years.

The sage thinks in generations beyond the
horizon. What patterns are going to end
with me? What wisdom can I pass forward?
What systems can I help redesign, so others
don't have to fight the battles I fought?
Where the keeper thinks of their children,
the sage thinks of their children's children.

This book exists because I'm beginning to
think that way. Certainly not perfectly or
completely, but enough to turn around and
offer what I've learned to those coming
behind me. In many ways, this book reflects
the spring of my sage identity. The infancy

of what will continue to grow in me for years to come from the warrior's effort and the keeper's seed.

The sage knows that the most important work often happens quietly. That the students who finally understand they don't have to sacrifice their health for success might not remember your name in ten years, but they'll remember the permission you gave them to choose differently. That the pattern you interrupt in your own life might echo forward in ways you'll never see.

That's enough. That must be enough, because the sage has learned that significance isn't measured in what you accumulate, it's measured in what you make possible for others.

These three identities, warrior, keeper, and sage, aren't rigid categories. You don't graduate from one to the next and never look back. Even now, I find myself slipping into warrior mode when stress hits. The old patterns are still there, carved deep by decades of use. The difference is that now I can notice it happening. I can recognize when I'm responding to a ghost instead of a present threat, and that's an important distinction. The warrior in me is resting, not dead. There may be times, hopefully rare, when it could be appropriate to bring the warrior back, but only temporarily and only as a specific remedy the keeper or sage sees as necessary. That is intention, not reaction.

You might discover you're living as a warrior in your career but a keeper at home. Or a keeper in your finances but a warrior in your health. These identities can coexist, and the work is recognizing which mode you're operating from in each domain of your life.

The framework isn't prescriptive. It's descriptive. It's a way to name what you're living so you can decide whether it still serves you.

If you're a warrior right now, exhausted and holding everything together through sheer effort, there's no judgment here. The warrior kept you alive and you should honor that, but when the conditions allow it, give yourself permission to set down some of what you're carrying.

If you're a keeper, learning to protect what matters and practicing the uncomfortable art of "enough", know that the transition takes time. The nervous system rewires slowly, so be patient with yourself.

And if you're approaching sage territory, or even just seeing glimpses of what that might look like, remember that the work isn't about perfection, it's about perspective. It's about turning around and extending a hand to those still fighting battles they should have let go of long before.

A Note on Age, Experience, and Time

You might be thinking, doesn't the keeper identity just come naturally with age and life experience? Don't people eventually calm down, gain perspective, and stop operating from constant urgency?

For some, that may be the case, but for others it may not be that simple. I lived as a warrior for over thirty years with no intention to stop before circumstances allowed recognition of the keeper to emerge. Age and accumulated experience may play a role, but it's not automatic.

It doesn't have to take that long, but for some people, it may never happen at all. I know people in their sixties and seventies who are still operating in warrior patterns, still unable to rest, still equating motion with worth. Age or experience alone doesn't create the shift.

What creates the shift is recognition combined with intentionality that allows change. You can be twenty-five and recognize the warrior operating in you. You can be sixty and just now see the pattern clearly for the first time. Hopefully, the circumstances of finding and reading this book leads to a eureka moment for you.

This book exists to give you the tools to identify and navigate these identities consciously, before spending decades waiting to discover them accidentally, or through a catastrophic event, or never discovering them at all.

If you recognize the patterns early and begin the transition intentionally, you could spend the majority of your years living as a keeper. You could build a life that doesn't require constant warrior vigilance before your nervous system has been shaped by it for decades.

That's the opportunity here. Not to eliminate struggle, that's not realistic, but to recognize when struggle has become habitual rather than necessary, and to choose differently when circumstances allow.

The warrior served you when you needed it. The keeper can serve you now, regardless of how old you are or how long you've been fighting. And the sage can serve others.

Chapter 11: Sacrifice While It's Voluntary

Throughout this chapter, I share examples from my financial advisory practice. These are real clients and real situations but identifying details have been altered to protect their privacy while preserving the patterns and lessons.

This is a phrase I use with every client I work with, one that's printed on my business cards and woven into nearly every financial plan I create. Sacrifice while it's voluntary. It sounds simple, maybe even obvious, but the resistance I encounter when people first hear it tells me it's neither.

The phrase challenges something we've been told our entire lives, that living for today and planning for tomorrow are opposing forces. That you're either enjoying life now or preparing for some distant future, but you can't do both. That presence and planning can't coexist.

That's not just wrong, it's dangerous.

The False Choice

"Live for today because tomorrow isn't guaranteed."

You've heard this. You've probably said it. It shows up in motivational posts, vacation photos, and justifications for purchases we can't quite afford but feel we deserve. And on the surface, it sounds liberating. Life is short, enjoy it while you can. You can't take it with you.

But underneath that philosophy, there's usually a fear we don't name.

The unspoken fear isn't that tomorrow won't come. Most of us, when we're honest, expect tomorrow to arrive. We expect many tomorrows. The real fear is that tomorrow will come, and we will not have planned for it.

That we'll wake up one day, older and more tired than we are now, and still working because we don't have a choice. Still sacrificing time and energy and presence to things we didn't choose. That the freedom we thought we were protecting by living for today will be the very thing we lose by failing to plan for tomorrow.

Involuntary sacrifice.

That's what we're really afraid of, not death. Not the sudden end of everything, but the slow erosion of choice. A future where we're trapped, still grinding and still exhausted, because we never built the margin that would have set us free.

Planning Enables Presence

Here's what I've learned, both from my own life and from watching hundreds of clients navigate this tension. You cannot truly live in the moment if you're constantly worried about tomorrow.

Presence requires security. Not wealth, not luxury, but the quiet confidence that the basics are handled, that bills are covered, and that an unexpected expense won't unravel everything. That you're not one crisis away from financial collapse.

When that security doesn't exist, "living for today" isn't freedom, it's avoidance. It's the warrior pretending motion equals progress while the foundation crumbles.

I know because I lived it. For years, I told myself I was focused on survival, on getting through each day, each month, each semester. I wasn't planning, I was reacting. And the constant state of reaction meant I was never actually present. Not with my family, not with my work, not even with myself.

Every moment was contaminated by the next crisis I couldn't see coming but knew was inevitable.

Future planning doesn't steal from the present, it protects it. When you know tomorrow is handled, maybe not perfectly, not luxuriously, but effectively, then you can truly be present without the background hum of motion that distorts everything.

Living for today and planning for tomorrow aren't mutually exclusive things, they're mutually beneficial. You plan for tomorrow so you can be present today. You sacrifice voluntarily now so you won't be forced to sacrifice involuntarily later.

The Keeper's Work

Voluntary sacrifice is the keeper's defining characteristic.

The warrior sacrifices too, but not by choice. The warrior sacrifices because survival demands it, because there's no other option, because the alternative is worse. The warrior's sacrifice is reactive, urgent, and driven by necessity.

The keeper's sacrifice is different. It's intentional and strategic. It's giving up something now, like time, money, comfort, or convenience, not because you have to, but because you understand that investment expands margins.

You sacrifice the third streaming service to fund the emergency fund that will keep the next car repair from becoming a crisis.

You sacrifice the promotion that would pay more but will cost you every evening and weekend, because you've done the math on what that time is really worth.

You sacrifice the immediate gratification of spending everything you earn, because you've tasted the freedom that margin creates and you want more of it.

None of this is deprivation. It's not suffering. It's not denying yourself joy or pleasure or comfort. It's making conscious trades based on what you value, rather than letting circumstance make those trades for you. Even in reading this book right now you've made a decision on how to spend your time. You've decided that that opportunity cost of this moment is worth what you've traded to be here.

The warrior sacrifices in survival mode, always behind, always catching up.

The keeper sacrifices from margin, always building, always protecting.

How Sacrifice Enables the Sage

Here's the part most people miss, the sage cannot exist without the keeper's voluntary sacrifice.

The sage, the version of you that contributes beyond your own survival, that builds things that outlast you, that shifts from "what do I need" to "what can I offer" only emerges when the foundation is secure.

You cannot give generously when you're drowning. You cannot think generationally when you're stuck in the immediate. You cannot build legacy when you're still trying to survive.

The keeper's work, the voluntary sacrifice that builds margin, systems, and security is what creates the platform the sage stands on.

I see this clearly now in my own trajectory. The warrior fought for survival. The keeper built the foundation. And now, slowly, the sage is beginning to emerge, not because I'm wealthy or because I've "made it", but because the keeper did the work that makes sage identity possible.

Teaching isn't just income for me anymore; it's part of my legacy. The financial planning I do with clients isn't just professional service, it's generational impact. The conversations I have with my kids about money aren't just practical instructions, they're pattern interruption.

None of that would be possible if I were still in warrior mode, still reacting, still sacrificing involuntarily.

The keeper protected the future, so the sage can live it.

What Happens When We Avoid Voluntary Sacrifice?

If you refuse to sacrifice voluntarily, you will eventually sacrifice involuntarily.

This isn't a threat and it's not moralizing, it's just math.

I worked with a client a few years ago, let's call him David, who earned around $150,000 a year. Good income. Stable job. But he was carrying about $40,000 in credit card debt and had no emergency fund.

When we sat down to build a plan, the math was clear, if he redirected $1,000 a month toward debt and savings, he'd be debt-free in four years with a solid emergency fund. The sacrifice was manageable through eating out less, postponing a vehicle upgrade, canceling subscriptions he rarely used.

He agreed to the plan, but then he didn't follow it.

Not because he couldn't. Because he didn't want to. He wanted to live his life now. He earned that income, and he deserved to enjoy it. The voluntary sacrifice felt like deprivation, so he avoided it. These were the very behaviors that left him with $40,000 in debt and no emergency fund in the first place

Three years later, his company went through a restructuring, and he was offered a buyout. He could take a severance package and leave or stay in a diminished role at reduced pay. He took the severance.

Without an emergency fund and still carrying the debt, that severance evaporated in a few short months. He had to take the first job he could find that included lower pay, longer commute, and work he didn't enjoy. The voluntary sacrifice he'd avoided became involuntary sacrifice, and it was far more painful than the modest budget adjustments we'd outlined.

The tragedy wasn't that he lost his job. Restructurings happen, believe me. The tragedy was that he'd had three years to prepare for exactly this kind of disruption, and he'd chosen not to.

Another client, I'll call her Sarah, came to me in a similar position. Mid-career, good income, some debt, no savings. The difference was in her response.

Sarah had watched her parents struggle through multiple job losses with no financial cushion. She'd seen what involuntary sacrifice looked like up close, and she was determined not to repeat that pattern.

We built a plan that required real trade-offs. She was driving a leased SUV that was eating $600 a month. She loved that vehicle, but she agreed to let the lease end and buy a reliable used car for cash. That freed up $600 immediately.

She adjusted her grocery spending, not by eating poorly, but by meal planning instead of grabbing convenience food. That saved another $300 a month. These were small changes but deliberately made.

With her new margin and some overtime dutifully applied to her debt, she was able to pay off around $30,000 in debt and built a six-month emergency fund in just over three years. Her base income hadn't changed. Her life didn't feel restricted. If anything, she felt lighter because the constant background anxiety about money had nearly disappeared.

Then her company also announced layoffs, and her position was eliminated and no severance was offered.

But this time, the outcome was different. She had margin. She had time. She could be selective about her next role instead of desperate. She took two months to find the right fit with better work, better culture, and similar pay. The layoff was still stressful, but it wasn't catastrophic. The voluntary sacrifice she'd made had protected her when involuntary circumstances arrived.

I've also seen clients who make progress, build margin, then relax too much and watch the warrior return.

A client, who I'll call Matt, eliminated $50,000 in debt in just over four years. Exceptional discipline. He'd built a solid emergency fund, and everything was working.

Then he started to drift. "I've earned the right to enjoy this", he told me. He upgraded his lifestyle incrementally. Nicer apartment. Better car. More frequent travel. None of it individually seemed excessive, but collectively, the margin he'd built slowly disappeared. This is lifestyle inflation.

Two years later, he was carrying $20,000 in new debt. Not back to square one, but close enough to feel it. The warrior he'd worked so hard to put behind him had quietly returned because he'd stopped making voluntary trade-offs.

The margin doesn't maintain itself; it requires continued intention.

Voluntary sacrifice isn't abstract. It's concrete decisions in specific categories. Here's how it looks in practice.

Housing

The warrior stretches to buy the biggest house the bank will approve. The keeper asks, how much house do we really need? We felt this in a major way after the four older kids moved out. We didn't really discuss it right away, but the thoughts emerged. Do we really need to stay in a house this big? Six bedrooms for just the three of us?

Voluntary sacrifice might mean staying in your current home instead of upgrading when your income increases. It might mean choosing the smaller, unassuming house instead of the bigger house that impresses from the curb. It might mean one fewer bedroom than you'd prefer because the mortgage payment protects your margin instead of consuming it. Or, as in our case, it may mean choosing to move to a smaller home when a bigger home no longer serves your needs.

A couple I worked with was pre-approved for a $450,000 mortgage. They could afford the payment, but it would be tight. Instead, they bought a house for $320,000 and that $130,000 difference translated to about $850 a month lower payment. They sacrificed the extra square footage and the "nice" neighborhood and in return, they built a six-month emergency fund in eighteen months and paid off their cars within three years. The house wasn't what they originally wanted, but it served their needs, and it fit their lifestyle. That's voluntary sacrifice, and it allows you to upgrade sooner and easier than if you maxed out your capacity earlier. That couple will be able to move into a $450,000 home soon with very comfortable margin because they delayed it a bit and didn't test their capacity.

Transportation

The warrior drives what signals success. The keeper drives what's reliable.

Voluntary sacrifice might mean keeping your current paid-off vehicle for a while longer instead of upgrading to something newer. It might mean buying a three-year-old certified pre-owned car instead of new. It might mean choosing the reliable Honda over the impressive luxury brand because the $400 monthly payment difference could fund your Roth IRA.

One client I had loved cars. Genuinely loved them. But he was carrying $35,000 in credit card debt while driving an $80,000 truck. We talked about the trade-off. He could keep the truck and stay in debt for another seven or eight years, or he could sell it and buy something reliable for $15,000 and be debt-free in two years.

He chose debt-free. He drove a ten-year-old Camry for three years. He hated it at first, but with the debt being gone and $25,000 in savings he was able to continue building, he bought a truck he really wanted later, but with cash. The voluntary sacrifice had a timeline and a purpose, and that made it sustainable.

Entertainment and Experiences

The warrior says yes to everything because rest feels like failure. The keeper says no to most things to protect space for what matters most.

Voluntary sacrifice might mean dropping from three streaming services to one. It might mean cooking at home six nights a week instead of eating out whenever you're tired. It might mean saying no to the expensive weekend trip with friends because you're focused on eliminating debt this year.

But here's the nuance, voluntary sacrifice isn't deprivation, it's prioritization.

One couple I worked with spent about $800 a month on restaurants and entertainment. When we built their plan, I didn't ask them to eliminate all of it, I just asked them to be more intentional. They kept $200 for what they genuinely valued, like having a date night twice a month, and redirected the other $600 toward their emergency fund. Six months later, they had $3,600 saved. The sacrifice was specific, and the benefit was tangible, and they never felt deprived because they didn't move from all to nothing.

Time

The warrior sacrifices time to earn more. The keeper sacrifices opportunities that may steal away time that has more important use.

This is often the hardest category because time sacrifices feel counterproductive. The adjunct class that pays $3,000 sounds like a great opportunity, but if teaching it requires committing to fifteen more hours a week and prevents you from being present with your family, the real cost isn't the hours, it's what those hours displace.

Voluntary sacrifice might mean not saying yes to every side hustle opportunity that would bring in extra money when your time is already stretched thin. It might mean not pursuing the promotion that comes with a 10% raise but a 20% increase in work hours. It might mean leaving work at 5:00 p.m. even when there's more you could do.

I had to make this sacrifice repeatedly. Every adjunct class I turned down felt like leaving money on the table. But saying no to one class meant saying yes to an evening with my wife. Time to write this book. Protecting space that allowed the keeper to emerge instead of forcing the warrior to keep running. When you're escaping poverty and debt, money feels like everything, but there are huge costs in operating that way. This is why it's so important to identify when that pattern no longer serves you.

The Pattern

Notice what these examples have in common. They're not about eliminating everything you enjoy, they're about choosing things you value most and protecting them by sacrificing what you can easily do without.

The warrior sacrifices indiscriminately, whatever it takes to survive. The keeper sacrifices strategically, whatever it takes to protect and build.

That distinction matters because voluntary sacrifice only works if it's truly voluntary and chosen with intention, not imposed out of fear.

If you don't sacrifice the small daily conveniences to build the emergency fund, you'll sacrifice something much larger when the furnace fails and you have to put it on a credit card at 24% interest. Then you'll be inconvenienced an a much more impactful way.

If you don't manage your time to allow meaningful connections and presence, you'll later feel the regret of time that can't be replaced.

If you don't sacrifice the convenience of reactive spending, you'll sacrifice the security that comes from knowing you can weather disruption.

And here's the critical part, when you avoid voluntary sacrifice long enough, it becomes an invitation for the warrior to return.

You might have started the transition to keeper. You might have built some margins, established some boundaries, and created some systems, but if you stop making voluntary trades, if you slip back into spending everything, ignoring maintenance, and avoiding the work that protects your future, the warrior will inevitably return.

Because involuntary sacrifice always calls the warrior back the moment circumstances force your hand, the moment you're reacting instead of planning, the moment survival mode kicks in again the warrior takes over, and everything you built as a keeper starts to erode.

I've seen this pattern dozens of times. Someone does the hard work to get out of debt, build an emergency fund, and establish boundaries, but then they relax.

They stop making voluntary trades. They drift back into old patterns and when the next crisis hits, and it always hits, they're right back where they started, except now they also carry the shame and regret of having "failed".

Making Voluntary Sacrifice Sustainable

If voluntary sacrifice is this critical, the question becomes, how do you sustain it without burning out?

Because here's the trap, voluntary sacrifice can slide into warrior territory if you're not careful. If it becomes performance. If it becomes punishment. If it's driven by fear instead of intention, those are warrior motives, not keeper motives.

Sustainable voluntary sacrifice requires three things:

1. Clarity about what you're building

The warrior sacrifices to survive. The keeper sacrifices to build. You need to know what you're building, not in vague terms like "financial security" or "a better life", but specifically what you are working toward.

What does enough look like? What does margin feel like? What becomes possible when you're no longer in survival mode?

If you can't answer these questions, voluntary sacrifice will feel like deprivation.

It'll feel like you're giving things up for no reason, and you'll stop.

When I ask clients these questions, the answers are often vague at first. "I want to feel secure", "I want to stop worrying about money." Those are valid feelings, but they're not easily measurable.

The keeper needs specifics. What does "secure" mean in dollars? Is it a six-month emergency fund? Debt-free except the mortgage? Enough invested that you could survive a job loss without panic? That's a big one.

If you can't quantify what you're building toward, voluntary sacrifice will feel like wandering in the dark. You'll sacrifice without seeing progress, and eventually, you'll stop.

2. Permission to adjust as circumstances change

Voluntary sacrifice isn't static. What you're willing to trade changes as your capacity grows, as your circumstances shift, as your values evolve.

The keeper I am now makes different voluntary trades than the keeper I started as a few years ago. Things that felt like essential sacrifices back then no longer matter now, while new sacrifices have become more important.

The framework stays the same, sacrifice voluntarily to protect your future, but the specific trades are always evolving.

Here's what adjusting looks like in practice. Maybe you started with an aggressive plan to pay off debt in three years. Then a health crisis arrives, and suddenly you need to redirect money toward medical expenses. The warrior panics or ignores the change until it becomes a crisis. The keeper adjusts, knowing this is a temporary hurdle.

Or maybe you've built the emergency fund you needed, and now your priority shifts. The voluntary sacrifice doesn't end here, it redirects. Maybe now you're building toward early retirement, or saving for a home, or funding a career transition. The trades change, but the practice of making them intentionally remains.

3. Recognizing that small, consistent trades beat dramatic gestures

The warrior goes big, cuts everything, commits to radical change, but burns out in six weeks.

The keeper makes small trades consistently, automates one payment, sets one boundary, says no to one thing, and then does it again tomorrow.

Voluntary sacrifice isn't about heroic effort. It's about sustainable intention.

Here's how you know if voluntary sacrifice is sustainable. It should feel intentional, not punishing. If you're white knuckling it through the process, and if every spending decision feels like deprivation, you've crossed into warrior territory.

The keeper makes trade-offs calmly. You're not sacrificing the third streaming service because you hate yourself or because you're bad with money. You're sacrificing it because you've decided the emergency fund matters more right now, and that decision was made from clarity, not panic. Many people find that most of the things they sacrifice don't return because once they've let go of them, their priorities upgrade.

If it starts to feel like punishment, pause and reassess. Make sure you're building something specific, not just restricting yourself out of fear.

The Permission You're Looking For

I know what some of you are thinking, "isn't this just delayed gratification dressed up in new language?" Isn't this the same "sacrifice now, enjoy later" philosophy that keeps people from ever actually living?

No, and the difference matters.

Delaying immediate gratification comes with the understanding that most sacrifices are temporary. The process of making these choices, however, is ongoing. It's how you build a sustainable and comfortable life over the long term. There is no finish line. You will always be trading resources between competing priorities. The question is whether you make those trades voluntarily with intention or whether circumstances make them for you.

Voluntary sacrifice isn't about delaying everything in your life. It's about designing it with purpose.

You're not sacrificing so you can live "someday". You're sacrificing specific things you value less to protect the things you value more. That's intentional living.

And here's the permission you might be looking for. Your voluntary sacrifice doesn't have to be noble. It doesn't have to serve anyone but you. If your reason for building margins is so you can quit your job and travel. Do it. If your reason for setting boundaries is so you can spend more time on hobbies that matter to only you. Do it. If your reason for sacrificing the illusion of wealth is so you can have the reality of freedom. Do it.

The keeper's work doesn't require external justification. It doesn't need to serve a higher purpose or benefit anyone beyond yourself. The sacrifice is voluntary, and the purpose is entirely yours to define.

Voluntary sacrifice is the mechanism.

It's how the keeper builds what the warrior can't. It's how you move from reactive to intentional. It's how you protect your future while living in your present.

And it's how the sage eventually emerges because you can't contribute beyond your own survival until your survival is no longer in question.

The next chapter will help you recognize where you are in this process. The chapter after that will give you practical starting points for making voluntary sacrifice real in each domain of your life.

But before we get to tactics and practices, I needed you to understand something very clearly. Sacrificing while it's voluntary isn't restriction, it's the key to freedom.

It's the difference between you managing your life and your life managing you.

The warrior doesn't get to choose, but the keeper does. And that choice, that voluntary sacrifice, is what changes everything.

Chapter 12: Recognition Before Change

If you've made it this far, something in these pages feels familiar. Not the specific details, because your story is your own, but the patterns within. The motion that never quite produces relief. The vigilance that persists even when the threat is gone. The exhaustion that feels earned, virtuous even, until one day it no longer does.

You might be sitting with discomfort right now. Maybe you've recognized yourself as a warrior who's been fighting long past the point when the war ended. Maybe you've seen glimpses of the keeper you could become, but the distance between here and there feels impossibly far. Maybe you're angry that it took this long to have language for what you've been living. Or maybe you see this in someone else and you're searching for a way to help them release unhealthy behaviors.

All of that is okay. It's more than okay, in fact, it's exactly right.

Recognition is often uncomfortable. It requires seeing clearly, and clear sight often reveals things we've been working very hard not to see. The life you've built, however successful it looks from the outside, might be costing you more than it's worth. The strategies that got you here may not get you where you want to be. You've been substituting motion for meaning, vigilance for safety, endurance for intention.

These realizations don't often feel like relief. They feel like loss, maybe even grief. Like standing in front of something you've been avoiding because once you acknowledge it, you can no longer pretend it doesn't exist.

Recognition often arrives quietly. Not as a dramatic revelation, but as a series of small moments that accumulate until they can't be ignored anymore.

It might feel like reading the descriptions of warrior behavior and realizing you've been holding your breath. Like seeing your own patterns reflected so accurately that you have to put the book down for a moment. You may be irritated by the realization.

It might also sound like a voice in your head saying, "Yep, that's what I've been doing". Not with judgment, but with the exhausted relief of finally having language for something you've felt but couldn't name. You may welcome the realization.

It might show up as resistance. An urge to argue with the framework, to explain why your situation is different and why these patterns don't quite apply to you. That resistance itself is recognition trying to break through a defense you've built to protect yourself from seeing clearly. You may resist the realization. I saw this one in myself especially.

Or it might arrive as grief. Not for what you've lost, but for the years you spent operating from a place of scarcity even when scarcity was no longer the reality. For the version of yourself that believed motion was the same as progress, that vigilance was the same as safety. You may grieve the realization.

In whatever way it arrives, recognition rarely feels triumphant, but it should feel honest. And honesty, after years of rationalization, can be heavy.

Here's what matters most. You're still here. You didn't close the book. You didn't dismiss the pattern as irrelevant or exaggerated. You kept reading. That alone tells me something important about you.

You're ready. Not to change everything immediately, and not to fix what's broken overnight, but ready to stop pretending that what you've been doing is still working as well as you've convinced yourself of.

Recognition is not failure. Recognition is the first act of agency. It's the moment when you stop being shaped entirely by circumstances and start choosing, consciously, what you'll carry forward and what you'll finally let go of.

Before you move into the self-assessment that follows, I want to give you permission for a few things.

Permission to be exactly where you are. You don't need to be further along than you are. You don't need to have figured this out sooner and you don't need to feel guilty about the time you spent operating from a warrior identity that no longer serves you. That identity kept you alive. It got you here. Honor that, even as you prepare to release it. Release any burden of shame you may feel. It doesn't serve you.

Permission to feel complicated emotions about what comes next. Change, even necessary change, involves loss. You might grieve giving up the warrior even as you know it's time to rest. You might resist the keeper even as you crave what the keeper offers. That's normal. That's human. You don't have to force yourself to feel ready before you actually are.

Permission to go slowly. This isn't a race. There's no deadline. The self-assessment that follows isn't a test you can pass or fail. It's a tool. A mirror. A way to see more clearly what's already true. You can take as much time as you need with it. You can come back to it later if today isn't the right day. You can stop and start as many times as necessary.

Permission to be honest. The only wrong way to do this is without honesty. If you're still deep in warrior mode and not ready to acknowledge it, the assessment won't help. If you're pretending to be further into keeper territory than you really are, you'll miss the insights that matter most. This work requires truth, even when, or especially when, the truth is uncomfortable.

I've worked with enough clients to recognize the common forms of resistance when they arrive. Maybe you're experiencing one of them right now.

"But I'm doing fine." You are. That's not the question. The question is whether "fine" is the same as "well". Whether functioning is the same as thriving. Whether you're living or just expertly managing survival mode.

"That's just how life is." For some people in extraordinary circumstances, this may be true. But for you? The person who fought their way out of something, maybe poverty or maybe something else, who built a career, who proved they could endure anything? You've already demonstrated you're capable of more than just accepting how things are. The question is whether you want to.

"I don't have time for self-reflection right now." That one's particularly insidious because it's often true. You don't have time. The warrior has built a life that doesn't allow time for examination. That's not an accident, that's the design, and as long as you're too busy to look clearly, you'll never be able to see what's actually happening. The warrior can help you here. Don't just find the time for this, make it. The warrior is very good with impossible schedules.

"My situation is different." Of course it is, the specifics always are. But the pattern? The identity underneath the specifics? That's remarkably consistent across very different lives. The details change, but the dynamic doesn't.

If you hear yourself in any of these, you're not just being resistant, you're being human. The resistance is information. It tells you that something matters here, something that's real enough to defend against.

The question is, what happens if you stop defending, just for a moment, and look?

You're about to look directly at patterns you may have been avoiding for years. That takes courage. Not the warrior's courage, which is about endurance and pushing through, but a different kind; the courage to stop, to see clearly, to admit that something needs to change even when you don't yet know how to change it, to be vulnerable.

That courage is already present in you. You've demonstrated it by opening this book and getting this far. That is a step, however small you may see it.

Why Recognition Comes Before Action

There's a reason this chapter sits between the framework and the assessment. Understanding the warrior, keeper, and sage identities intellectually is one thing, but recognizing which identity is driving your life right now is something else entirely.

Most self-help books rush past this step. They move immediately from concept to prescription. "Here's the problem, here's the solution, now go fix it." But that approach fails more often than it succeeds because it skips the most important work. The honest recognition of where you are, not where you wish you were or think you should be.

You cannot change what you haven't acknowledged. You cannot release what you're still pretending doesn't exist. And you cannot develop a keeper identity while the warrior continues to operate, unexamined and uncontested.

Recognition is positive, not normative. It names what is, without immediately demanding what should be. That distinction matters because judgment shuts down honesty. The moment you start evaluating yourself, asking "am I doing this right?", "am I far enough along", "why haven't I figured this out yet", you stop seeing clearly. You start performing for an imagined audience instead of truthfully assessing your actual state. There is no audience anymore. This is personal, internal.

The self-assessment that follows is designed to help you see clearly. Not to grade you. Not to compare you to anyone else. Not to tell you you're failing. Just to help you recognize, with precision, which identity is operating in which domains of your life right now.

Because here's what I've learned, the identities aren't always consistent. You might be a warrior at work but a keeper at home. A keeper with money but a warrior with your health. A sage in how you mentor others but a warrior in how you treat yourself.

Recognition requires that level of nuance. It requires looking at your life domain by domain, pattern by pattern, and asking honestly, which identity is in control here?

That question isn't about right or wrong. It's about truth. And truth, once seen clearly, creates possibility. Not certainty and not a guaranteed path forward, just possibility.

The space to choose differently if you decide that's what you want.

I've seen this play out with clients who came to me at similar points in their lives. Both high earners, both carrying debt they couldn't explain given their income, and both exhausted.

One recognized the pattern immediately. "I've been doing this for fifteen years", he said. "I just didn't have words for it." That recognition didn't fix anything instantly, but it created the space to start making different choices. Small ones at first, then larger ones.

The other spent our entire session explaining why his situation was unique, why the framework didn't quite apply, why he just needed to work a little harder for a little longer and then things would ease up. Two years later, he was still saying the same things. Still waiting for the relief that never came. Still defending. It was a very relatable and recognizable "someday" pattern.

Recognition doesn't guarantee change, but denial guarantees stagnation.

What Honest Self-Assessment Requires

Before you move into the assessment itself, let's be clear about what it asks of you.

It requires time. Not in hours, but more than a few distracted minutes. You'll need space to think, to reflect, to sit with questions that might not have immediate answers. Treat this seriously. Not because it's a test, but because it matters. Find a time when you won't be interrupted. When you can give this your full attention. When you're not already exhausted or overwhelmed or rushing to the next thing. This is a making time effort, not a finding time task.

It requires honesty. This is for you, not for anyone else. No one is grading your answers. No one is judging whether you're warrior enough or keeper enough or on the right timeline. Not being honest here only impacts you and your ability to live a better life.

If you're not ready to be honest, if you're still too invested in a particular self-image or too afraid of what you might find, that's okay. Come back to this later. There's no shame in recognizing you're not ready yet. That recognition itself is valuable.

It requires sitting with discomfort. Some of the questions will land uncomfortably. They're designed to. Not to hurt you, but to help you see past the stories you've been telling yourself. The discomfort means the question is touching something real. Don't rush past it. Sit with it. Let it reveal what it needs to reveal.

It requires resisting the urge to fix anything immediately. You'll be tempted, when you see a pattern clearly, to immediately start problem-solving. To jump to solutions and to strategize how to change things right now. Resist those urges. Recognition comes first, understanding comes second, and only then does change become possible and sustainable.

The warrior wants to fix everything immediately. The keeper knows that seeing clearly is the foundation everything else is built on. Give yourself permission to just see first. The action steps will come, but not yet.

Preparing for What Comes Next

The self-assessment in the next chapter is structured around 6 life domains: work, money, health, relationships, time, and rest. For each domain, you'll be asked to reflect on specific patterns and behaviors that indicate which identity is currently in control.

This isn't a quiz. There are no points to tally. No score that determines whether you pass or fail. The assessment works through honest reflection, not through right answers.

Here's how to approach it effectively:

Create the right environment. Find a quiet space. Turn off notifications. Give yourself at least 30-45 minutes of uninterrupted time. Have something to write with and something to write on, whether that's a journal, a notes app, or blank paper. You'll want to capture your thoughts as they emerge, not just answer in your head and move on.

Read each question fully before answering. Don't skim and don't assume you know what's being asked based on the first few words. Some questions have multiple layers. Some ask you to compare current state to past state. Some ask about feelings, not just behaviors. Pay attention to what's being asked. Your focused presence is not only required, but also crucial.

Answer for your current reality, not your aspirational one. This is critical. The assessment asks where you are now, not where you want to be or where you think you should be. If you're still deep in warrior mode, say so. If you're somewhere in between warrior and keeper, name that. If different domains show different identities, acknowledge the inconsistency. That's normal. That's valuable information.

Notice your resistance. If a question makes you defensive or dismissive or angry, pause there. That reaction is data. It's telling you something. Don't ignore it or rush past it. Sit with it and ask yourself, why is this question uncomfortable? What am I protecting by resisting it?

Don't try to fix what you find. I'm going to say this again because it is important, recognition comes before change. The assessment is diagnostic. Its job is to help you see clearly, not to prescribe action. You'll be tempted to jump immediately into problem-solving mode. "Okay, I see the pattern, now how do I fix it?" Stop. Just see it first. Understand it. Let it settle. The action steps come later, after you've fully acknowledged what's true.

Be specific. Vague answers produce vague insights. If a question asks how you spend your time, don't just say "I'm busy". Specify what busy means. How many hours? Doing what? For whom? To what end? The more specific you can be, the more useful the assessment becomes.

Write it down. Even if you think you can hold your insights in your head, write them down. There's something about putting words on paper (or screen) that makes patterns more visible. It also gives you something to return to later. Recognition deepens over time. What you see clearly today might reveal even more a week from now, but only if you've captured it.

Expect discomfort, but not despair. This process is designed to reveal truth, and truth isn't always comfortable. You might see patterns you don't like. Behaviors you're not proud of. Identities you've outgrown but are still clinging to. That's okay. That's normal. That's the point. But if the discomfort becomes overwhelming, if it tips into despair or shame or hopelessness, just stop. Take a break and come back to it when you're steadier. This work requires honesty, but it doesn't require self-flagellation.

One More Thing Before You Begin

The self-assessment is not the end of the work. It's the beginning.

What you discover in the next chapter won't fix anything by itself. Recognition is necessary, but it's not sufficient. You'll need to decide what to do with what you find. That decision comes later, after you've sat with the insights, after you've let them settle, after you've considered what change would require.

But none of that is possible without this step. Without looking clearly at where you are. Without naming the identity that's been running your life. Without acknowledging the gap between how you're living and how you want to live.

That's what you're about to do. Not because you're broken, not because you've failed, but because you're ready to see what's true and

to consider, maybe for the first time,
whether what's true is also what you want.

Take your time. Be honest. Trust the
process.

When you're ready, turn the page.

Chapter 13: Self-Assessment - Where Are You Now?

This assessment is designed to help you see clearly which identity is operating in different areas of your life. There are no right or wrong answers. There are no scores to calculate. There is only honest reflection.

Take your time with each domain. Write down your answers. Notice where the questions make you uncomfortable, that discomfort is information. Notice where you want to defend or justify your responses, that impulse is also information.

Remember, you're not being graded, you're being asked to see clearly.

Work and Career

Your relationship with work reveals identity patterns more clearly than almost anything else. The warrior equates work with worth, motion with value, and exhaustion with responsibility. The keeper works with intention, protects boundaries, and knows when enough output is enough.

1. How many hours did you work last week?

Count everything. Your primary job, side work, work you brought home from the office, work you thought about during "off" hours, emails you answered on weekends. Be honest about the total.

Now ask yourself, was this a week typical, or was it unusually busy? If you said, "unusually busy", when was the last typical week and what did it look like? How many hours? Go for typical, not extraordinary.

2. When was the last time you said no to a work opportunity or request?

Not, "I would have said no but it was required", but an actual no to a project, a committee, extra hours, or additional responsibility. Something you wanted to say yes to but chose not to.

If you can't remember the last time, that's your answer.

3. What happens in your body when you think about taking a full day off?

Not a weekend, those don't count for most people, but a random Tuesday or Wednesday. A full day with no work, no checking email, no "just quickly reviewing" anything. This is taking a day off, outside of your regular scheduled days off. If you don't work Monday through Friday, adjust this response accordingly.

Do you feel relief? Anxiety? Guilt? Does your mind immediately start listing reasons why that's not possible right now? Does your chest tighten? Do you feel excited or threatened?

Your body's response tells you which identity is in control.

4. If your job disappeared tomorrow, who would you be?

Not what would you do for income, that's a different question, but who would you be? How much of your identity is tied to your work title, your productivity, your schedule, and your professional role?

Don't simply name your non-work identity. Parent, sibling, spouse, etc. That will still exist in addition to any role. Who are you in place of your professional role? If the answer is "I don't know" or "I'd be lost", the warrior is running this domain.

5. Do you take your full lunch break?

This does not include eating at your desk while working or scrolling your phone while eating, but an actual break away from your workspace doing something that isn't productive.

If the answer is "I don't have time" or "there's too much to do", notice that. The keeper makes time. The warrior feels that they can't afford to.

6. How do your colleagues describe you?

Not how you want them to describe you, but how they actually do. Are you "always available"? "The one who gets things done"? "Never says no"? "First one in, last one out"?

If your professional identity is built on endless availability and capacity, the warrior is still in charge.

Money

How you relate to money reveals whether you're operating from scarcity or margin, from vigilance or trust, from fear or intention. The warrior monitors constantly, never fully trusts that enough exists, and equates financial safety with constant attention. The keeper builds systems, trusts what's been built, and knows the difference between prudence and hypervigilance.

1. How many times did you check your bank balance or credit card balances in the past week?

Not for specific reasons like planning a purchase, verifying that one specific payment cleared, or reconciling your budget, but just checking. Opening the app to look at the numbers and making sure everything is still okay.

If the number is more than three times, ask yourself why. What are you protecting against? What would happen if you didn't check? Did you check out of need or habit? Did you change anything based on what you found when checking?

2. When you have an unexpected expense, what's your first emotional response?

Not your practical response, which is figuring out how to pay for it, but your emotional response. The feeling that arrives before the problem-solving kicks in.

Panic? Immediate mental scrambling? Despair? Anger? Resentment? Resignation? Or was it relative calm, knowing you can absorb it?

The warrior goes immediately into crisis mode. The keeper might be annoyed but isn't destabilized.

3. Do you have autopay enabled for recurring bills?

If yes, how long did it take you to feel comfortable with that? Do you still check to make sure the payments went through even though they're automated?

If no, why not? What would happen if you weren't manually controlling every transaction? What are you afraid you'd miss?

The warrior needs to maintain control. The keeper can delegate to systems.

4. What's your emergency fund balance right now?

Not what you wish it were. Not what you're working toward, but the actual number today. This is easy-to-access money in a local bank savings account. This is not retirement money or anything else intended for other reasons that could be used, but money held for the sole purpose of using it in an emergency.

If you don't have one, or if it's less than one month of expenses, the warrior is running your financial life, especially if your income is high. Margin isn't about how much you earn; it's about the space between earning and obligation.

5. When was the last time you spent money on something you wanted but didn't need and felt okay about it?

Not guilty and not justified through elaborate reasoning, just okay. You wanted it, you could afford it, you bought it, you moved on. Did you pay for it using credit or did you have money designated for the purchase? Did you regret the purchase later?

If you can't remember the last time, or if every non-essential purchase comes with guilt or requires permission from someone else, the warrior is still in control. The keeper can spend intentionally without self-punishment.

6. How much of your financial behavior is driven by fear versus intention?

This one requires honesty. Are you saving for a specific goal, or saving because you're afraid of what might happen if you don't? Are you avoiding debt because you've built a keeper framework, or because the warrior is still standing guard?

Fear-based financial behavior looks responsible from the outside, but it feels different on the inside. The warrior's discipline comes from threat. The keeper's discipline comes from choice.

Health

Your body keeps the score. How you treat your physical and mental health reveals whether you're still operating from warrior endurance or have moved into keeper care. The warrior pushes through pain, ignores signals, and treats the body as a tool to be used. The keeper listens, responds, and recognizes that sustainable performance requires recovery.

1. When was the last time you went to the doctor for a regular checkup, not because something was wrong?

Preventive care, annual physicals, and routine screening. Not urgent care, not "I finally couldn't ignore this anymore", and not "my spouse made me go".

If it's been more than a year, or if you can't remember, the warrior is running this domain. The keeper maintains the system before it breaks.

2. How many hours of sleep did you get last night?

Not how many hours you were in bed, but how many hours you slept. Was that typical, or are you catching up from deficit? Was your sleep restful and effective, or poor quality? Is that typical?

Now ask, is that amount sustainable long-term? Are you chronically running on less than your body needs and telling yourself you've adapted?

The warrior believes sleep can be optimized away. The keeper knows it can't.

3. What does your body do when you're stressed?

Headaches? Jaw clenching? Stomach and digestive issues? Back pain? Insomnia? Skin problems? Hair loss? Frequent emotional breakdowns? Elevated heart rate that persists after the stressor is gone? High blood pressure?

Can you name the specific physical manifestations of stress in your body, and more importantly, do you pay attention to them, or do you push through them?

The warrior ignores the body's feedback. The keeper listens and responds.

4. When was the last time you exercised, not because you "should", but because you wanted to?

Not punishment for eating and not compensation for sitting all day. Not grinding through a workout to check a box. Movement that felt good. That your body enjoyed. That left you energized rather than depleted. When was the last time you exercised as part of doing something fun?

If exercise only exists as obligation or penance, the warrior is still in charge. The keeper moves for pleasure and health, not performance or guilt.

5. Do you take your full sick days when you are sick?

Do you show up anyway and work through illness? Do you answer emails from bed when you should be resting? Do you feel like you are letting people down by being human and needing recovery time? Do you fully check in, taking advantage of technology to work remotely that day instead of resting?

The warrior can't afford to stop, even when the body demands it. The keeper understands that working through it extends illness and reduces long-term capacity.

6. What's your relationship with pain?

Do you push through it? Ignore it? Medicate it so you can keep going? Or do you investigate it, rest when needed, and treat pain as information rather than inconvenience?

If your default response to physical discomfort is work around it rather than address it, the warrior is running your health. The keeper knows that ignored pain rarely goes away, but compounds instead.

Relationships

The warrior's relationships are often transactional or deprioritized, and functional rather than nourishing. Time with people becomes another obligation to manage rather than a source of connection and recovery. The keeper protects relational time, shows up present rather than distracted, and understands that relationships require investment that doesn't always look productive.

1. When was the last time you had a conversation with someone you care about that wasn't rushed?

Not catching up while doing something else. Not a quick phone call squeezed between obligations. Not half-present while thinking about your next task. An actual conversation where you were fully there.

If you can't remember, or if it's been more than a week, notice that. The warrior doesn't have time for unhurried connections. The keeper makes time.

2. How often do you cancel or reschedule personal plans because of work?

Not emergencies, but regular work that came up or otherwise needs to be done. Plans with friends, family, your partner, your kids that get moved because work takes priority.

If this happens more than once a month, the warrior is still running your priorities. The keeper protects relational commitments with the same seriousness as professional ones.

3. When you're with people you care about, where is your phone?

In your hand? On the table face-up? Are you checking it frequently, or is it put away, silenced, out of sight?

When it buzzes or rings, do you check it immediately, or do you let it wait? Are you comfortable with it silenced entirely?

The warrior can't fully disconnect. The keeper can be unavailable to work in order to be available to people.

4. Do the people closest to you feel like they have your attention?

Not just do you spend time with them; that's a vague quantity. Do they feel seen, heard, prioritized, or do they feel like they're competing with your work, your phone, your mental to-do list?

If you're not sure, ask them for their honest feedback. Their answer will tell you which identity is influencing your relationships.

5. When was the last time you initiated connection, not out of obligation, but because you wanted to?

When you last called a friend just to talk or planned something with your partner that wasn't logistical. Spent time with your kids that wasn't about managing their schedule. Reached out to someone you care about with no agenda to cover.

The warrior's relationships become another thing to maintain. The keeper's relationships are important sources of satisfaction and fulfillment, not drains on capacity.

6. How do you respond when someone needs you but it's inconvenient?

Do you show up anyway? Resent the interruption? Calculate whether they "deserve" your time based on what they've done for you recently? Feel guilty either way, for saying no or for saying yes?

The warrior keeps score and operates transactionally. The keeper gives from connection, not from obligation, and can say no without guilt or resentment when boundaries require it.

Time

How you relate to time reveals whether you're living from urgency or intention, scarcity or sufficiency. The warrior is always racing against time, filling every available hour, and treating unscheduled space as wasted opportunity. The keeper understands that margin in your schedule is as important as margin in your budget.

1. How much unscheduled time did you have in the past week?

Not time you filled with chores or caught up on work. Not time spent scrolling on your phone or watching TV mindlessly out of exhaustion, but actual open time. Time with no agenda. Time you could have used for anything or nothing. Did that make you feel uneasy or like you were missing something? There's always something that could be done, but are you ok with not doing those things or are you distracted by those feelings?

If the answer is less than 10 hours in a full week, the warrior is running your schedule. The keeper protects unstructured time.

2. When was the last time you were bored?

Not tired, not frustrated by waiting, but truly bored. Sitting with nothing to do and no immediate plan to fill the space.

If you can't remember, that's your answer. The warrior can't tolerate empty time. The keeper knows boredom creates space for unexpected thoughts and recovery.

3. How far in advance is your calendar filled?

Look at the next four weeks. How many of those days have virtually every hour accounted for, including time traveling between obligations? How many have built-in buffer time between commitments? How many are completely open? Would it be difficult to pencil in something unexpected, like an invitation to an event?

If your calendar is packed solid weeks in advance, the warrior is in control. The keeper builds margin into the schedule itself; not just hopeful that free time will appear.

4. What happens when something takes longer than you expected?

Do you immediately start calculating what you'll have to cut or compress? Do you feel anxiety rising? Does your mood shift? Or can you adjust without crisis?

The warrior's schedule has no slack. One delay creates a cascade. The keeper's schedule has buffer built in. Delays are absorbed, not catastrophic.

5. Do you routinely commit to more than you can reasonably accomplish in a day?

Look at your to-do list or your mental sense of what "needs" to get done today. Is it realistic, or is it a warrior's wish list that would require perfect conditions and no interruptions to complete?

The warrior overcommits by default. The keeper plans realistically and protects capacity.

6. How do you feel about doing nothing?

Guilty? Wasteful? Anxious? Uncomfortable? Like you should be doing something productive? Or do you feel peaceful? Restful? Like it's exactly what you need?

If doing nothing feels like failure, the warrior is still defining your relationship with time. The keeper knows that rest isn't earned, it's required.

Rest and Recovery

Rest is where the warrior and keeper identities become most visible. The warrior treats rest as something to be earned, minimized, or optimized. The keeper understands that rest is fundamental, not a reward for productivity, but a requirement for sustainable living, and can be enjoyable.

1. When was the last time you took a full day to rest with no agenda, no productivity, and no catching up?

Not a weekend where you ran errands and did chores. Not a sick day. Not recovering from being pushed past your limit. A day you chose to rest simply because rest matters.

If you can't remember, or if the idea itself feels impossible or indulgent, the warrior is running this domain.

2. Do you feel guilty when you rest?

When you're sitting still, reading for pleasure, taking a nap, watching something you enjoy, is there a voice saying you should be doing something more productive?

The warrior can't rest without guilt. The keeper rests without apology.

3. What does your body do when you finally stop?

When you finish a big push, complete a major project, or finally have space to rest what happens physically? Do you immediately get sick? Crash hard? Sleep for 12+ hours? Or do you transition smoothly because you've been maintaining yourself all along?

If your body collapses the moment after you stop pushing, the warrior has been running you past sustainable limits. The keeper maintains a pace that doesn't require collapse.

4. How do you spend your mornings before obligations begin?

Are you rushed from the moment you wake up? Checking email the moment you're out of bed? Racing through a routine to get to the next thing? Or do you have space? Time to ease into the day? Do you have moments of quiet before demands begin?

The warrior wakes up already behind. The keeper protects the transition into the day.

5. When you're exhausted, what do you do?

Push through with caffeine and will power? Tell yourself you'll rest later (but later never comes)? Feel resentful that you can't keep going? Or do you stop, rest, recover, and let your body and mind catch up?

The warrior's default is endurance. The keeper's default is response. Exhaustion is information, not weakness.

6. What's your relationship with vacation or time off?

Do you take it at all? Use all your days? Or do you hoard them, feel guilty using them, work through them, or treat them as emergency backup rather than necessary recovery?

When you do take time off, can you fully disconnect, or do you check email, stay available, work "just a little" because you can't let go?

If taking personal time off feels like a luxury that you can't afford rather than a necessity you must protect, the warrior is still in charge. The keeper knows that time off isn't optional, it's foundational.

What You've Just Done

You've looked directly at six major domains of your life and asked which identity is running each one. That takes courage and honesty.

By now, you've likely noticed patterns. Maybe the warrior is running most domains. Maybe you're a warrior at work but a keeper at home. Maybe you're making progress in some areas while others remain stuck.

All of that is information. All of it is useful.

Don't rush to fix what you've found. Sit with it first. Let the patterns become clear. Let yourself see fully before you start problem-solving. Expand on your answers if something pops into your head. Treat it like a journal for a bit. Come back to it a second time and skim your answers to see if anything needs an update.

Over the next few days, notice what comes up for you. Notice where resistance appears.

Notice where you want to defend your warrior patterns or justify why change isn't possible right now. That resistance is also information.

The assessment has done its job if it's helped you to start seeing things differently, more clearly, that's the foundation. Everything else, the decisions about what to do with what you've found, the changes you might choose to make, the identity shifts you might pursue, all come after the pattern recognition.

You've taken the first step and that matters more than you might realize.

Chapter 14: What To Do with What You've Found

If you've completed the self-assessment honestly, you're probably sitting with some uncomfortable realizations right now. Maybe you discovered the warrior is running more of your life than you thought. Maybe you saw patterns you've been avoiding for years. Maybe you're angry that it took this long to see clearly or feel overwhelmed by how much needs to change.

All of that is normal and all of that is okay.

Before we talk about what to do, let's talk about what not to do. These are the five most common mistakes people make when trying to shift from warrior to keeper.

Trying to change everything at once. Monday morning arrives and you decide no more checking the budget obsessively, quit the side hustle, start resting more, say no to commitments, and completely restructure your life, then by Friday you're exhausted and back to old patterns. The warrior identity is built over years, maybe decades. The keeper can't be installed overnight. Choose one behavior to shift. Just one. This month, check your budget weekly instead of daily. That's it. Nothing else needs to change yet. Small, sustainable shifts compound over time. Wholesale overnight transformation doesn't last.

Beating yourself up for warrior relapses. You checked your bank balance three times today even though you didn't need to. You immediately think, I'm failing at keeper. I'll never get this right. Here's the truth, shame strengthens the warrior because it calls on all the warrior's strengths to avoid it. The warrior demands perfection, requires constant performance, punishes mistakes. Using warrior tactics to eliminate the warrior doesn't work. Instead, notice moments of regression without judgment. Ask why. "I checked three times today. What was I worried about? What did I think checking the balance would solve?" That curiosity is keeper thinking. That awareness is progress, even when the behavior hasn't changed yet.

Comparing your timeline to others. Someone else paid off their debt in eighteen months, while you're in year three. Someone else transitioned to keeper quickly, while you're still struggling. You think "I'm doing this wrong" but your warrior identity has unique history, depth, and triggers. It was shaped by circumstances and experiences specific to you. Their timeline isn't your timeline. Compare yourself only to the past you. Ask yourself, am I more keeper than I was six months ago? If yes, that's progress. That's all that matters. And here's some extra credit for you, just asking the question and observing if you've made progress is keeper behavior! So, the answer is yes, simply by virtue of asking the question.

Expecting immediate emotional relief. You paid off the debt or left the job or made the change. You expect to feel free, light, relieved, but instead, you still feel vigilant, anxious, and on edge. You think something's wrong. Nothing's wrong. The spreadsheet changes faster than your nervous system. Your circumstances shifted, but your body is still catching up. The warrior identity lives in your nervous system, not just your behavior. It takes time for your body to learn that the threat is gone, that rest is safe, that you don't need to stay on high alert anymore. The identity crisis after the situational crisis is normal. You're not broken; you're transitioning.

Skipping the recognition step. You read about the framework and immediately jump to action. You start making changes without understanding which identity has been running your life. This rarely works long-term because you can't change what you haven't acknowledged. The sequence matters. Recognition, then understanding, then intention, then action. In that order. Spend time with recognition first. Spend one week just noticing when the warrior appears. No changes yet, just awareness. Where does it show up? What triggers it? How does it feel in your body? Recognition creates space for intentional change. Without it, you're just using warrior tactics to fight the warrior.

These mistakes are normal, and I hesitate to even call them mistakes. Knowing they exist helps you recognize them faster and adjust the course instead of thinking you've failed.

But here's what comes next, and it's not what you might expect.

You don't need to fix everything immediately. In fact, trying to overhaul your entire life at once is exactly what the warrior would do. The warrior sees a problem and attacks it. Throws effort at it. Commits to dramatic change through sheer force of will. And usually, within a few weeks or months, the warrior burns out and everything snaps back to how it was before. Hopefully this theme is getting through to you by now.

The keeper works differently. The keeper knows that sustainable change happens slowly, through small shifts that compound over time. Through intention, not intensity. Through building systems that make the new way easier than the old way. Where the warrior is all gas and no brakes, the keeper is cruise control.

This chapter isn't a prescription. It's not a step-by-step program that promises results if you just follow the formula. What it offers instead is guidance and practical starting points for the transition from warrior to keeper, tailored to the six domains you just assessed.

You might not need all of it. You might need to focus on one domain for six months before touching another. You might discover that some shifts happen naturally once you address the leverage point that's been holding everything else in place.

That's fine. That's expected. That's how this works.

The warrior wants a battle plan. The keeper wants a map.

Start Where You Are

Pick one domain, but not the one that feels most broken or most urgent, those are often warrior traps that lead to burnout. Pick the one that feels most ready. The one where you can already see what small shift might make a difference. The one where you have some ability to make changes.

For some people, that's money. Once you automate a few payments and stop checking your balance multiple times a day, the mental space that frees up cascades into other areas.

For others, it's rest. Once you protect one full day of actual rest per week, your body stops operating in crisis mode and everything else becomes more manageable.

For others, it's work. Once you say no to one extra project and the world doesn't end, saying no the next time becomes easier.

There's no right starting point. There's only your starting point, the domain where change feels possible right now, not "someday" when conditions are perfect, which is never.

Here's the other thing about leverage points, they're often smaller than you think. You don't need to quit your job to shift your work identity. You don't need to eliminate all debt to shift your money identity. You don't need to train for a marathon to shift your health identity.

You need one honest boundary to begin. One automated system. One morning when you don't check email as soon as your feet hit the floor. One conversation where you're fully present instead of half-distracted.

Small shifts sustained over time. That's how the keeper builds a life that doesn't require constant warrior vigilance.

Domain-Specific Starting Points

What follows are practical first steps for each domain. These aren't comprehensive programs, they're entry points. Small shifts that create space for larger changes later.

You don't need to do all of these. Pick one or two that resonate with where you are right now or identify your own that may be more specific to your needs. The exact details may not relate to your life perfectly, but you'll get the idea and be able to adjust based on your needs.

Work and Career

Set one non-negotiable boundary, not ten. One. Maybe it's no email after 7pm. Maybe it's taking your full lunch break three days a week. Maybe it's saying no to the next committee invitation. Pick one boundary that feels both important and achievable, then protect it for 30 days.

The warrior will tell you that this one boundary doesn't matter, that it won't make a difference, that you can't afford it. Ignore that voice. The boundary itself isn't the point. Proving to yourself that you can set and hold a boundary is the point.

Stop checking emails first thing in the morning. Give yourself the first 30-60 minutes of your day before work takes over. Eat breakfast. Move your body. Sit with coffee and silence. Do anything except immediately plugging into work's demands.

This shift changes your nervous system's baseline. Instead of waking up already in reactive mode, you start the day with agency and purpose and a pace that you have set. That tone carries through the rest of your hours.

Track your actual work hours for two weeks. Not what you think you're working, but what you're truly working. Every email answered, every task completed, every minute spent thinking about work during "off" time. Just observe and record. Don't try to change it yet.

The warrior operates in vague urgency. The keeper operates on data. Once you see the actual numbers, the patterns become undeniable. That clarity creates space for intentional change.

Money

Automate one recurring payment, just one. If you're already checking to make sure automated payments have gone through, stop checking for 30 days. Let the system do its job without your constant monitoring.

This practice isn't about the payment itself; it's about learning to trust systems instead of substituting vigilance for security. Start small and build trust gradually.

Reduce balance-checking to once per week, not zero, that might trigger too much anxiety. But once per week, on a specific day, at a specific time. Make it a ritual, not a compulsion. If once doesn't feel possible right now, try twice.

Every time you feel the urge to check between your scheduled times, pause. Ask yourself, what am I protecting against right now? What do I think will happen if I don't check? Write down those fears. Notice how rarely catastrophic scenarios actually occur.

Spend money on one want without guilt. Something small that won't hard on your finances. Something you don't need but genuinely want. Budget for it, then go buy it. Practice moving on without elaborate justification or self-punishment.

The keeper can spend intentionally without guilt. This practice builds that muscle. Start small, maybe a book, a fancy coffee, a meal out. The amount doesn't matter; the permission does.

Health

Schedule one preventive health appointment. A wellness physical, dental cleaning, vision check, or whatever you've been putting off because "nothing's wrong yet". Make the appointment, then go to the appointment.

The keeper maintains the system before it breaks. This single action signals a shift from reactive to proactive health management.

Protect 7-8 hours for sleep, three nights this week, not seven nights, that might feel impossible right now. Choose three nights and block the time. Treat it as non-negotiable. Notice what had to shift to make that happen and notice how you feel the next day.

The warrior believes sleep is negotiable. The keeper knows it's foundational. You can't think clearly, regulate emotions, or make good decisions when you're chronically sleep-deprived. This isn't indulgence, it's basic maintenance.

Listen to one pain signal instead of pushing through it. If your back hurts, rest it instead of loading it with more weight. If you have a headache, stop working and hydrate instead of taking ibuprofen and continuing. If your body feels tired, cancel the workout and sleep instead. Choose one signal to respond to and notice what happens. Notice that responding to your body's signals doesn't make you weak, it makes you sustainable.

Take a 30 minute walk with no particular destination. Observe how you feel during and after your walk. Let your mind wander away from obligations and see how your thinking changes. If possible, do this two or three times this week, then build up to daily if you can.

Go outside. Not for any specific purpose, but just to breathe the fresh air and see and hear nature. If you don't live in a place where you're likely to see or hear nature sounds, visit a place nearby where you can. Fifteen or twenty minutes in a green space can have quite a positive effect on your cortisol levels. Breathe, look, and listen, then take note of what you experienced.

Author's note: nothing presented here should be construed as medical advice. All health-related questions, concerns, and changes should be discussed with a healthcare professional first.

Relationships

Have one fully present conversation this week. Phone away and laptop closed. No mental to-do list running in the background. Choose one person you care about and give them 30 minutes of your complete and undivided attention.

This will feel harder than it should. Your mind will want to wander. You'll feel the pull to check your phone. Notice those urges, let them pass, and return to presence. This is the practice that leads to better habits.

Stop checking work communications during one evening or weekend activity with people you care about. Dinner, a movie, or a walk. Whatever you're doing together, be fully there. Silence your phone. Put it in another room if you need to.

The warrior stays tethered to work even during "off" time. The keeper can disconnect to be fully present. Start with one activity and build from there.

Initiate connection with someone you care about with no agenda. Call a friend just to talk. Ask your partner about their day and actively listen. Spend time with your kids doing something they want to do, not something productive.

The keeper's relationships are sources of life, not obligations to manage. This practice rebuilds that orientation.

Time

Block two hours of unscheduled time in the next week. Put it on your calendar and protect it like you would a meeting. When the time comes, don't fill it with plans. Don't optimize it. Just let it remain open.

You might read. You might walk. You might sit and think. You might do nothing at all. The point isn't what you do, it's learning to tolerate open time without filling it compulsively.

Say no to one commitment you would normally feel obligated to say yes to. A project, a request, or an invitation. Something you have the capacity to do but don't want to do. Practice saying, "Thanks, but I need to pass on this one."

The warrior says yes by default because motion equals value. The keeper protects capacity by saying no strategically. One no. Notice that the world keeps turning.

Build fifteen-minute buffers between meetings or commitments for one week. Avoid booking your schedule back-to-back. Create space and breathing room. Time to transition from one thing to the next without rushing. Let your mind disconnect from one thing before connecting to the next.

The keeper builds margin into the schedule itself. This practice shows you what that feels like and how much more sustainable it is than running late all day.

Rest and Recovery

Take one full day of rest in the next two weeks. Not a weekend where you catch up on chores. A day with no agenda and no productivity built in. A day you choose to rest simply because rest matters.

This might be the hardest shift on this entire list. Every survival instinct will protest that you can't afford it, that too much needs to be done. Do it anyway. Observe what happens. The work will still be there tomorrow, but you'll be more capable of doing it after resting.

Stop working when you're sick. Next time you're ill, not just tired, but sick, take the full sick day. Don't answer emails from bed. Don't work "just a little" because you're home anyway. Rest completely and unapologetically. You are not available during this time.

The keeper understands that working while ill extends illness and reduces long-term capacity. This isn't weakness, it's maintenance.

Practice doing one thing purely for enjoyment this week. Not exercise because you "should". Not reading for professional development. Something you do just because it brings you pleasure. A hobby you've abandoned. A creative outlet. A show you want to watch but have put off or that you've ignored while doomscrolling on your phone.

The keeper knows that rest can be enjoyable, not just necessary. This practice rebuilds that relationship.

Common Obstacles

Even small changes meet resistance. Some of that resistance comes from the outside, from systems, expectations, or other people who benefit from your warrior patterns, but much of it comes from inside. From your own nervous system, which has been trained for years or decades to operate a certain way and doesn't update just because you've decided things should be different.

Here's what to expect, and how to navigate it.

When Others Resist Your Boundaries

The people around you, such as colleagues, family, and friends, have adapted to your warrior availability. When you start setting boundaries, some of them will push back.

Your boss might question why you're not answering emails at 9:00 pm anymore. Your family might resist when you're not available to solve every problem immediately. Your colleagues might express concern that you're "checking out" when you start taking your full lunch break.

This resistance isn't usually malicious, it's adaptive. They've built their own systems around your unlimited availability. When you change, their systems have to adjust too, and that creates friction.

How to navigate this:

Be clear and consistent, but within the requirements of your job. That's an important line to define. What are the true requirements of your job, and what are self-generated expectations? Don't apologize for boundaries or over-explain them. "I don't check work email after 7pm" is complete. You don't need to justify it with your life story or convince anyone it's reasonable. State the boundary and hold it.

Expect testing. People will test new boundaries to see if you're serious. The first time you don't respond to a late-night email, someone will escalate it the next day as if it was urgent. Hold the boundary anyway.

After a few iterations, they'll learn the new pattern.

Distinguish between accommodation and erosion. True emergencies happen and boundaries can flex when necessary, but "this feels urgent to me" isn't the same as "this is actually urgent". The keeper knows the difference. Don't let every request become an emergency that requires you to abandon your boundaries.

Accept that some people won't adjust. A few people in your life might never accept your boundaries. They'll continue to pressure, guilt, or manipulate you into action. You can't control their response. You can only control whether you maintain the boundary anyway.

The warrior apologizes for boundaries and caves under pressure. The keeper holds boundaries with calm firmness, even when it's uncomfortable.

When You Backslide

You will backslide. This is guaranteed.

You'll set a boundary and then violate it. You'll automate a payment and then check it obsessively anyway. You'll protect rest time and then fill it with work because something came up. You'll slip back into warrior patterns under stress, exhaustion, or when old triggers activate.

This isn't failure, it's just part of the process.

The nervous system doesn't rewire in a straight line. You take two steps forward and one step back, or sometimes one step forward and two steps back. The pattern over time matters more than any single day or event.

How to navigate this:

Notice without judgment. When you catch yourself in warrior mode again, don't spiral into self-criticism, just notice it. "I'm doing the thing again. The warrior is back." Observation without judgment creates space for course correction.

Ask what triggered the slip because backsliding isn't random. Something activated the old pattern. A stressful deadline. A conflict. An unexpected expense. Financial pressure. Identify the trigger so you can prepare differently next time.

Return to practice without drama. You missed three days of your boundary. Okay, done, start again today. You checked your bank balance fifteen times this week instead of once. Okay, done, return to practice tomorrow. The warrior sees backsliding as evidence of unworthiness and failure. The keeper treats it as data and keeps going.

Celebrate that you're noticing things. Six months ago, you wouldn't have even recognized you were in warrior mode. You didn't have language for it then. Now you can see it happening, sometimes in real-time, and name it. That awareness is progress, even when the behavior hasn't fully changed yet.

Progress isn't linear and the direction matters more than the pace.

Guilt and Discomfort

As you shift toward keeper patterns, you'll feel guilt, and maybe a lot of it.

Guilt when you rest. Guilt when you say no. Guilt when you automate something instead of controlling it manually. Guilt when you're unavailable. Guilt when you prioritize your own needs.

This guilt doesn't mean you're doing something wrong. It means you're doing something different. Your nervous system was shaped by environments where rest was dangerous, where saying no had consequences, where self-prioritization was selfish. The guilt is the old system resisting the new one.

Name it for what it is. "This is warrior guilt. I feel it because I'm changing, not because I'm doing something wrong." Language creates distance and distance creates choice.

Sit with discomfort. Don't try to fix it or make it go away immediately. Feel the guilt and hold the boundary anyway. Feel uncomfortable and rest anyway. The discomfort diminishes with repetition, but only if you don't cave in to it every time.

Distinguish between guilt and harm. Guilt is an internal state; harm has an external impact. You can feel guilty without harming anyone. Most of the time your boundaries don't harm others, it just inconveniences them or requires them to adjust. That's okay. That's allowed.

Give it time. The guilt that feels overwhelming today will feel manageable in three months and barely noticeable in six. Your nervous system is recalibrating. Trust the process.

The warrior avoids guilt by never resting or setting boundaries. The keeper acknowledges the guilt and does what's right anyway.

The Pull Back Under Stress

Here's the pattern you need to expect, you'll make progress, build some keeper habits, start to feel more sustainable, and then something stressful will happen, like a deadline, a crisis, an unexpected expense, or a conflict and suddenly you'll be right back in warrior mode.

Full hypervigilance. Checking everything constantly. Working around the clock. Ignoring your body's signals. Saying yes to everything. Abandoning every boundary you've built.

This reversion under stress is normal. It's how the nervous system works. When threat is detected, it reaches for the most practiced response. For you, that's the warrior. That pattern has kept you alive. It's deeply engrained and is the "fight" part of your "fight or flight" response. Of course you will return to it under pressure.

This is slightly different than backsliding, which is when you make a change and then revert to your old system. Pulling back is a reaction to some external event.

How to navigate this:

Expect it. Don't be surprised when stress activates old patterns. Build it into your model of how this works. "When I'm stressed, I'll default to warrior mode. That's normal, and it's not permanent."

Shorten the duration. Early in the transition, you might stay in warrior mode for weeks after a stressful event. As you practice, that duration shortens to a week, then a few days, and eventually just hours. The goal isn't to never revert, it's to return to keeper mode faster each time with clarity and intention.

Use stress as information, not evidence. The fact that you reverted to warrior mode under stress doesn't mean the keeper changes aren't working. It means stress happened. This is a different data point. Don't let one stressful week erase three months of progress in your mind.

Build explicit recovery practices. After a high-stress period, intentionally return to keeper practices. Block a full day of rest. Reconnect with people. Sleep. Move gently. Don't just hope you'll bounce back, actively rebuild the margin that the stress depleted.

The warrior expects perfection and interprets any slip as total failure. The keeper expects imperfection and treats slips as part of the process.

You're not trying to eliminate the warrior entirely. You're learning when the warrior is appropriate (rarely) and when the keeper serves you better (almost always). That discernment takes time. It takes practice. It takes falling back into old patterns and consciously choosing new ones, again, and again, and again.

That's not failure. That's the work.

Building Keeper Systems

The warrior relies on willpower. The keeper builds systems.

Willpower is a finite resource. It depletes throughout the day. It also weakens with stress, exhaustion, or decision fatigue. When you rely on willpower alone to maintain new patterns, you'll succeed when conditions are good and fail when they're not.

Systems don't require willpower when they can run automatically. They make the right choice an easy one. They remove decisions from the moment and bake them into the structure.

This is how the keeper makes change sustainable. Not through constant effort, but through intentional design.

Automation: Let Systems Do the Work

Automation is one of the keeper's most powerful tools. Anything that can run without your active involvement, should.

Financial automation:

· Recurring bills on autopay

· Automatic transfers to savings on payday

· Retirement contributions deducted before you see the paycheck

· Debt payments scheduled automatically

· Automatic prescription refills

The warrior monitors every transaction manually because control feels safe. The keeper automates the essentials and only reviews periodically. This frees enormous mental bandwidth.

Work automation:

· Email filters that sort incoming messages, so your inbox isn't chaos

· Calendar blocks for focused work that repeat weekly

· Auto-responses during off-hours that set clear expectations about availability

· Templates for recurring communications

The warrior recreates everything from scratch every time. The keeper builds it once and lets it run.

Health automation:

· Recurring calendar appointments for preventive care (annual physical, dental cleanings, etc.)

· Medication reminders if needed

· Meal planning systems that reduce daily decision-making

· Regular sleep and wake times that don't require nightly negotiation

The more you automate, the less willpower you need. The less willpower you need, the more capacity you have for higher priority things that require your attention.

Boundaries: Design Constraints That Protect

Boundaries aren't restrictions, they're design constraints that protect what matters.

The warrior sees boundaries as limitations on capacity. The keeper sees boundaries as frameworks that enable sustainability.

How to design effective boundaries:

Make them specific and observable. "Better work-life balance" isn't a boundary, it's a wish. "No work email after 7pm on weekdays" is a boundary. It's specific and measurable. You can tell whether you're holding it.

Build them into systems, not willpower. Don't rely on remembering to stop checking email, turn off work notifications after 7pm. Don't rely on remembering to take breaks, set calendar blocks that allow them. Design the system so the boundary holds even when you're tired or stressed.

Start smaller than feels necessary. If you want to stop working on weekends, start with Saturday mornings. If you want to take full lunch breaks, start with three days a week. Set small boundaries you can effectively hold and build the muscle for larger ones later.

Communicate your boundaries clearly once, then hold them consistently. You don't need to re-explain your boundaries every time they're relevant. State them once, then demonstrate through consistent action that they're real.

Expect them to feel uncomfortable at first. Boundaries should create some friction. If they don't, they're not effective boundaries, they're just descriptions of what you were already doing. The discomfort means they're working.

The warrior's boundaries are reactive, set in crisis and abandoned under pressure if they exist at all. The keeper's boundaries are structural, designed in advance and maintained through systems.

Environmental Design: Make the Right Choice the Easy Choice

Your environment shapes your behavior more than your intentions do. If your environment is designed for warrior patterns, keeper behavior will require constant effort. If your environment is designed for keeper patterns, keeper behavior becomes natural.

How to design your environment:

Remove friction from desired behaviors. Want to exercise more? Put your workout clothes next to the bed so they're the first thing you see. Want to read before bed instead of scrolling? Charge your phone in another room and keep a book on your nightstand. Want to rest on weekends? Delete work apps from your phone or use app timers to limit access.

Add friction to undesired behaviors. Want to stop checking work email constantly? Log out after each session so you have to consciously log back in. Want to reduce impulsive spending? Remove saved payment methods from shopping apps.

Want to stop working late? Shut down your computer at a specific time and physically remove it, preferably to another room.

Create visual cues for new patterns. The keeper uses environmental reminders that don't depend on remembering everything. A sticky note on your bathroom mirror that says, "Just breathe." A calendar block titled "Unscheduled time - protect this." A phone background that reminds you of what matters.

Batch decisions to reduce daily willpower drain. The warrior makes the same decisions every day about what to eat, when to work out, whether to take a break. The keeper decides once and builds a system. Meal planning on Sundays. Workouts at the same time every week. Breaks at the same intervals every day.

The easier you make keeper behavior, the less willpower it requires. The less willpower it requires, the more sustainable it becomes.

Accountability: Structure That Supports Change

Some changes are easier to maintain when someone you trust knows you're making them.

This isn't about external pressure or judgment. It's about creating gentle support structures that makes backsliding slightly harder and progress slightly more visible.

How to build useful accountability:

Tell one person about a change you're making. Not everyone, and not every change. One person you trust with one specific shift you're working on. Ask them to check in occasionally, not to police you, but to notice you.

Join or create a small group focused on similar transitions. This doesn't need to be formal. A few friends who are also learning to set boundaries. A small online community. People who understand the struggle and can relate to the discomfort.

Track visible progress in a way you're likely to go back to. A simple spreadsheet, a habit-tracking app, or a physical calendar where you mark days you held a boundary. The format doesn't matter. What matters is making progress visible to yourself.

Celebrate small wins explicitly. The warrior only notices when things go wrong. The keeper marks when things go right. You held a boundary for a full week? Note it. You automated one of your payments and didn't check it for three days? Acknowledge it. Small celebrations reinforce new patterns.

The warrior changes alone through force of will. The keeper builds support structures that make change more sustainable.

Systems aren't a one-time build. They evolve as you do. What works when you're early in the warrior-to-keeper transition won't be what you need six months later. The keeper adjusts systems as circumstances change, capacity grows, and new patterns stabilize.

The goal isn't to build perfect systems. The goal is to design systems that reduce the daily willpower required to live as a keeper instead of a warrior. Systems that make the sustainable choice the default choice.

That's how change becomes permanent. Not through endless effort, but through intentional design.

Closing

You've just read practical guidance for shifting from warrior to keeper identity patterns across six life domains. You've learned about obstacles you'll face and systems you can build to make change sustainable.

But here's what matters most, you don't have to do all of this. You don't even have to do most of this. You just need to start somewhere, no matter how small.

Pick one domain. Pick one small shift. Do that thing for 30 days. Notice what happens. Notice what changes, not just externally, but internally. Notice how your nervous system responds. Notice whether the guilt diminishes. Notice whether the space you create starts to feel necessary instead of indulgent, then decide what comes next. Maybe you deepen the change in that same domain. Maybe you add one small shift in a different area. Maybe you pause and consolidate what you've built before adding anything new.

There's no timeline and there's no right pace. There's only your pace, the speed at which change feels sustainable rather than heroic.

The warrior would try to implement everything at once, burn out within weeks, and interpret the inevitable collapse as personal failure. You know better now. You know that sustainable change is built slowly, imperfectly, with obstacles and course correction.

The warrior tracks obsessively. The keeper tracks intentionally. Here's what accountability looks like without shame.

Monthly check-in

One question: Which identity was most active this month? Not good or bad, just observation. Write it down. Warrior, keeper, or mix. Over time, patterns emerge. Maybe warrior returns during busy seasons. Maybe financial stress triggers it. Maybe family conflicts bring it back. The pattern itself is information. You're not judging it; you're learning from it. And depending on where you are on this path, maybe you'll observe the sage identity making an appearance in some areas.

Quarterly assessment

What's one keeper behavior I've adopted? Even if it's small. Maybe you checked the budget weekly instead of daily. Maybe you said no one time without spiraling into guilt. Maybe you rested for an afternoon without feeling like you were losing ground. Name it. Celebrate it. The keeper needs acknowledgment too, just differently than the warrior. Then ask, what's one area where the warrior is still running the show? Not fixing it immediately, just to see it clearly.

Annual review

Am I moving toward keeper, or do I remain stuck in warrior? If you're stuck, what's blocking the transition? Fear? Identity? Lack of support? Resources? If you're moving, what helped? What hindered? Adjust course for next year based on what you've learned. Maybe you caught a glimpse of the sage developing in some area. How exciting! Make a note of this, reflect on it, and feel it.

When to ask for help

If the warrior is causing active harm, often seen as a health crisis, relationship breakdown, or financial danger, get professional help now. If you're stuck and genuinely can't see why, ask someone you trust to reflect back to you what they observe. If you need practical guidance, find it. But if you just need time, give yourself time. Keeper sometimes takes years to fully develop. That's not a problem to solve, it's a reality to accept.

Building keeper support

Find people who understand the transition. A partner or spouse who's read this book. A friend who's also moving from warrior to keeper. A therapist who can help with identity work. A financial advisor who respects keeper boundaries instead of pushing warrior tactics. You don't need a team; you just need someone who sees what you're building and supports the pace it requires.

The keeper tracks to learn, not to punish. That difference changes everything.

You know that the goal isn't to eliminate the warrior entirely, it's to recognize when the warrior is operating and choose consciously whether that's appropriate for the moment. Most of the time, it won't be. Most of the time, the keeper will serve you better, especially when you realize you're already past whatever threat you were escaping.

Some moments still require the warrior's strength. True emergencies and short-term pushes that that have some real level of necessity and have clear end points. Situations where endurance is genuinely necessary, not just habitual.

The difference is knowing which is which. That discernment, knowing when to push and when to rest, when to say yes and when to protect your boundaries, when motion is productive and when it's just motion, that's what you're building.

It takes time and practice. It takes more patience with yourself than the warrior ever had.

But you're not the warrior anymore. You're becoming the keeper, and the keeper knows that the most important work often looks like rest and reflection, not output. That the most productive thing is sometimes doing nothing. That rest isn't only earned, it's required. That enough is a real threshold, not just something people say.

You've taken the assessment. You've seen the patterns. You've read the guidance. Now the only thing left is to begin.

Not perfectly. Not all at once. Just one small shift. One boundary. One system. One choice that prioritizes sustainability over performance.

That's enough. That's how this works.

The work ahead isn't easy, but it's worth it and you're ready.

Understanding the Danger Zones

Throughout this book, I've referenced danger zones, those moments where the patterns become particularly deceptive. Let me clarify them explicitly:

Danger Zone 1: High income, high debt, narrow margin (Chapters 4-5)

This is where things look successful from the outside. You're earning well, the bills are paid, systems are functioning, but underneath there's no slack. Every unexpected expense triggers stress. You're one disruption away from collapse. The danger here is that functionality is masquerading as stability, and you confuse managing the load with having margin.

Danger Zone 2: Post-debt, before identity shift (Chapter 9)

This is the quieter risk that comes after debt is eliminated. The pressure lifts and credit cards now sit empty. The systems you built under duress no longer feel necessary. Comfort starts to look like safety. This is where people slip, not through crisis, but through the gradual erosion of the vigilance that got them out. The danger here is backsliding before the new identity solidifies, before the keeper replaces the warrior.

Both zones require awareness and intention. Neither resolves itself through time alone.

Epilogue: What I Hope You Keep

If nothing else, I hope this book steadies you. Not with answers or certainty, but with recognition. The intention here was never to outline change. It was to uncover an identity, to name a pattern, and to offer language for something that may have felt heavy or all too familiar. I hope you feel seen. I hope you feel validated. I hope you feel relief that you're not alone and that you're not doing anything wrong. This is about acknowledgment, not judgment.

If you recognize yourself somewhere in these pages, somewhere in the motion, in the vigilance, in the way effort quietly became an identity, then you've already done the most important work. You've seen the pattern, and once you see it, you can decide what to do with it. But there's no urgency to deploy that realization. Sitting with it is enough for now.

This was never a story about money. Money was just the language the problem spoke in. The real work was learning how to stop living as though danger is always imminent long after the danger had passed. It was learning to recognize when discipline had turned into compulsion, when endurance had replaced intention, and when motion had crowded out meaning.

I spent years believing that safety came from staying ahead. From working harder. From carrying more. From never letting anything fall behind. What I eventually learned is that safety doesn't come from motion, it comes from margin. Margin to think. Margin to choose. Margin to rest without fear. Margin to absorb normal life without panic. Margin shows up in money, yes, but it also shows up in time, health, relationships, and agency, and without it, even success feels fragile.

You cannot spreadsheet your way out of a nervous system shaped by scarcity and hypervigilance. That requires slower, quieter, and deep personal work. What does that work look like? It looks like deliberate choices instead of frantic motion. It looks like collaboration that's effective, not competitive. It looks like focused time to think with large blocks of time not held captive by low-priority demands. It looks like meetings that matter instead of meetings that could have been emails. It looks like engagement that's personal instead of transactional. It looks like environments where people are genuinely interested in your success, not just your output. Most importantly, it looks like having the space to recognize what no longer serves you and the permission to let it go.

Should you expect immediate change, or will it take longer? I think it's both immediate and long-term. The immediate change can simply be that you've opened your mind to the possibility of a different way of living. That's no small thing. That shift in awareness changes what you notice, what you question, and what you're willing to tolerate. The long-term change will look like updated, more effective behavior leading to material improvements in your life. But that takes time. Months not days, years not weeks, and that's okay.

If this book has done its work, then maybe quietly, somewhere deep in your own life you'll recognize a tired warrior in you. What should you do with that recognition? Sit with it. Let the thoughts linger. Take account of how it has helped you in the past and how it might be restricting you today. Resist the urge to feel fault. There is nothing to fault. This is not judgment. This is honesty. The warrior kept you alive. That identity served you. It may have been the only thing that could have carried you through what you faced, but you must be able to recognize when the battle is over.

In the early stages being a keeper means protecting yourself, your time, and your boundaries. Much of establishing the keeper identity is about creating boundaries and deciding what gets your attention, what gets your energy, and what gets your "yes". The keeper is not passive, however. The keeper is intentional. That's a big difference.

There's a risk, of course, that you'll try to rush the transition. That you'll try to force yourself out of warrior mode and into keeper mode immediately. But that urgency, that forcing, naturally calls on the warrior in practice. It defeats the purpose. The most common mistake people make after recognition is blaming themselves for time lost to unnecessary identity. They focus on the "what ifs" had they made this realization sooner. Don't do that. You can't reclaim the past. You can only redirect the future.

How do you maintain the necessary discipline without falling back into vigilance? Boundaries. "I don't need to check my balance five times a day." "Receipts can be updated in the budget weekly, not daily." "I have an account for the unexpected. I don't need to rework the entire budget to accommodate a minor deviation." These small shifts from constant monitoring to trusting the system you've built are what the keeper practices.

What happens when you inevitably slip back into old patterns, because you will? Remember this; success rarely comes without failure. You haven't failed until you give up. The warrior taught you endurance. The keeper teaches you grace, and most importantly, that includes grace for yourself.

Let me say something about hope. If you're still in your own version of Chapter 5, if your body is pushing back, if the limits are appearing, or if you sense something has to change but don't know what, here's what I can offer. Every day is a fresh opportunity to write a new story for yourself. No matter where you're starting, there is a path forward, and there are probably far more people ready to support you and celebrate your growth than you realize.

The path is different for everyone, so don't sabotage yourself with superficial comparisons. Just as with your own story, people only know what they're shown, and the truth beneath the surface is entirely personal. You don't have to have it all figured out today. You don't have to fix everything at once. You just have to be willing to see the patterns, and once you see them, you can decide what comes next.

What I wish someone had given me earlier is permission. Permission to acknowledge that escape is okay but doesn't need to be extreme. Permission to sit with fear without letting it consume me. Permission to be vulnerable instead of perpetually resilient. I will give you that permission now, if you need it. You don't have to be the warrior anymore. Not because the warrior failed, but precisely because the warrior succeeded.

The threat you were running from is behind you now. You've put distance between yourself and what you feared most. It's safe to stop running. It's safe to turn around and see how far you've come. It's safe to rest. The people in your life who love you deserve your presence, and above all, you owe yourself presence. You've earned it.

Bleeding for Ghosts

"Bleeding for ghosts" is a metaphor for how the past continues to drain us. Ghosts are anything from your past that is not part of your present, except in a way that they're still draining you. Financially, emotionally, or in any other way. Past financial hardships. Unsustainable work volume. Relationships that were hopeless. Even something as simple as the interest paid on credit card charges for purchases that are now long forgotten. Those purchases are ghosts, but you're still bleeding for them.

When we stop bleeding for ghosts it looks like peace. It looks like agency over your time and thoughts. It looks like waking up and not immediately scanning for threats. It looks like a day where you're not constantly braced for impact. It looks quiet, almost boring at times when you're used to constant motion.

When you are finally able to sit with the quiet presence of your own thoughts. When you have space between life's events and your own mind, body, and soul. When you move with purpose rather than reaction. You will find that happiness is found in the margin.

The Work That Remains

Stopping the bleeding isn't the end of the story. It's the beginning of something else.

The keeper protects what the warrior built. The keeper creates margins, maintains boundaries, and trusts systems. That work is essential and it's the foundation for everything that comes after.

But the sage, the identity I'm still learning to inhabit and express, does something different. The sage looks outward. Not from obligation or depletion, but from overflow. From having built enough margin that giving doesn't threaten the foundation.

I see this most clearly in my teaching. Not the performance of teaching, but the actual investment in students who remind me of myself at twenty. The ones working multiple jobs. The ones sacrificing sleep and health because they believe struggle proves commitment. The ones who don't yet know that endurance and worth are not the same thing.

I can't make their choices for them, but I can offer language for what they're living. I can help them recognize patterns before those patterns turn into decades of mismatched identity. That's sage work, not prescribing answers, but helping others recognize questions they didn't know they could ask.

The same is true for my children. I didn't always get it right. I worked too much during their early years. I modeled endurance when I should have modeled rest. But I'm also showing them something different now. What it looks like to say no to opportunities that erode margin. What it looks like to prioritize presence over performance. What it looks like to stop running a marathon and enjoy a nice, leisurely walk instead.

They're still watching, not just what I say, but what I do. Whether I practice what I teach. Whether the keeper identity is real or just another performance. I think the strongest indication they have that these identities are real is how I interact with their own children, my grandchildren. In my eyes, having grandchildren is having the opportunity to love your children all over again, but with better insight into yourself.

That's the generational work, not perfection, but course correction. Breaking cycles that span lifetimes. Choosing differently when circumstances allow and modeling that choice for those who come after.

I won't see all the outcomes of that work. The student who learns to set boundaries at twenty-five instead of fifty might not remember my name in ten years. The pattern I interrupt in my own life might echo forward in ways I'll never witness. My grandchildren will inherit a different baseline because I chose to stop bleeding for ghosts.

That has to be enough, because significance isn't measured in what you accumulate. It's measured in what you make possible for others.

The sage knows that the most important work often happens quietly. That legacy isn't about being remembered, it's about what you leave behind in the lives you touch. The changes you brought about in others and in the world that you affected.

The questions you help others ask. The permissions you offer. The patterns you interrupt.

I'm not fully there yet. The sage identity is still aspirational for me, not achieved. But I'm learning to give without keeping score, learning to mentor without an agenda, and learning to trust that the seeds I've planted will grow, even if I'm not there to see the results.

That's the journey ahead. Not just for me, but maybe for you too, when the time is right. When the keeper has done its work and margin is no longer something you're building, but a permanent part of your life.

Author Q & A: Beyond the Framework

After completing this manuscript, I shared it with early readers, family, friends, colleagues, and people who watched parts of this journey unfold. Their questions were insightful, sometimes challenging, and often touched on aspects of the framework I hadn't fully explored in the main text.

Rather than weave these answers throughout the book, I've collected them here. Some are practical. Some are personal. Some I'm still working through myself. Think of this as the conversation we might have if we sat down over coffee after you finished reading, the questions you'd ask, the details you'd want to know, the parts of my experience that might help clarify yours.

Part 1: Current Life Reality

What does your budget look like now, after becoming debt-free? Has your relationship with money changed?

Today the budget is much more relaxed with options and slack. I still plan everything to the penny, but there are far fewer revisions and much less monitoring. I usually update the budget once a week now as opposed to daily or more in the past.

My relationship with money has changed, in that before I felt controlled by money. So much of my time and energy were spent in pursuit of it, while now I see money as a tool to be used more strategically. I'm no longer earning to get away from something, I'm earning to build strategically.

What surprised you most about post-debt life? Any keeper behaviors that are still hard?

The biggest surprise was just not knowing what to do and having the experience of an unfamiliar identity. The crisis I've mentioned is entirely related to identity. I didn't know who I was and that is confusing and frightening. There are plenty of resources available to help you get out of debt, but far fewer to help you adjust to it outside of the spreadsheet.

Are there still moments when warrior thinking returns? What triggers it?

Yes, there are times when I see an opportunity, such as with an adjunct class that needs a professor, that I feel an automatic desire to take it even if I don't need to. I also frequently still consider cost over quality when buying things.

What does margin buy in daily life? What can you do now that you couldn't do before?

The biggest thing is that I can simply relax. I have control over my time that I've never had before in my entire life. I've gone hiking, I've returned to school for a PhD, and here...I've written this book.

My daily life now starts with slow, quiet mornings that are no longer rushed. I enjoy coffee in my kitchen, not in the car. I make my breakfast rather than picking it up from a drive-thru window. In terms of money, I'm now able to enjoy an unplanned purchase without feeling the dread of what the budget will look like after.

How does living on a teaching salary (without healthcare management income) really feel? Is it genuinely sustainable?

It's not only sustainable, but I have more discretionary money now than I've ever had in my life. I still teach some adjunct classes, but even with that additional commitment it feels like I'm working at 50% of my previous workload.

Yes, teachers are generally underpaid for what they provide, but I would not describe my income as low or even average. I do well, and with a few extra online classes I'm back to almost 80% of my previous salary. But, when you compare that to feeling like I'm only working 50% as much, I'll take that every time! And it's not just that it feels like 50% less work, it truly is 50% less, and

maybe more than that when you consider
that I was carrying over a full-time teaching
load in addition to my manager role
previously.

Are you still working on your PhD? How
does that fit with the keeper identity?

I am in my first year of the PhD program as
of this writing. I do find that I sometimes
need to access the warrior mode to meet
deadlines with schoolwork, but that is the
exception. Generally, I find that the process
itself supports my keeper identity, knowing
that I'm building something far greater than
a credential. It often crosses into sage
territory where I am considering what my
research and work may accomplish beyond
personal benefits.

Does your wife still work at your former
employer? How has that dynamic evolved?

My wife does still work for my former
employer. I find myself less and less aware
of what's going on there, and when she tells
me about some new project or policy it
mostly feels foreign now. I still hear from
my former colleagues occasionally and
genuinely enjoy connecting with them, but I
no longer feel connected to my former
employer or my former career.

Part 2: Framework Clarifications

Are you in sage territory yet? Honestly, where are you in the transition?

I'm definitely still in the keeper identity. I've just realized these identities over the past two years or so, and they are not clean breaks from one to the other. So, I would say I sometimes see the warrior operating when needed, although it's far less often, while I'm living as the keeper on a daily basis with glimpses of the sage appearing occasionally.

I suspect the keeper identity will be years long in development and growth. Why wouldn't it be if the warrior identity could go on unchecked for over 30 years? I also suspect that the longer you're operating as a warrior, the longer it takes to develop the keeper and finally become the sage.

What would it take to reach the sage identity? Is it about having more margin? More time?

I don't like to think of the sage as requiring more of anything. That goes entirely against this process. The sage will emerge in its own time as the keeper builds the foundation and the lessons learned become habits and then later default standard behaviors.

If you're doing sage things, what do they look like?

Planning for my children's and grandchildren's futures and the legacy I want to leave them. My kids may be adults now, but they will always be my kids, and I will always watch over them. Also mentoring where I can, including life lessons in my classes when there's extra time, and writing this book.

Can someone skip keeper and go straight from warrior to sage?

I don't know how a warrior to sage transition could be possible. The keeper builds a foundation and boundaries. Those are necessary before the sage can exist and the warrior cannot do that. The sage doesn't spend its time the way the keeper does.

And remember, we're not replacing one identity with another. They all exist simultaneously, but how we live reflects which one is in charge. We let the warrior rest, we let the keeper protect, and we let the sage provide a legacy.

What's the difference between "building margin" and "living simply" or "minimalism"?

Living simply or minimally doesn't give any indication of change or margin. Someone can live simply or minimally for years with no change in their margin, but building margin is an intentional path and it often requires scaling back lifestyle a bit. The important thing to remember is that it's not permanent and the benefits on the other side are life changing.

The ironic thing, however, is that many people do not return to an excessive lifestyle after building margin. Many people enjoy living lighter once they've done so.

Do you still drive used cars? What's your relationship with material possessions now?

My wife and I both drive new vehicles now. Mine is the first truly new vehicle I've ever owned in my life. I don't work on cars anymore, not because I can't, but because I protect my physical health and time margins now, so we enjoy the warranty protection that comes with the new vehicles, and I enjoy relaxing while the oil is being changed, or the brakes are being replaced.

Does the keeper identity mean frugal? Can the keeper buy nice things?

The keeper is intentional. There's nothing wrong with frugal, but that's different than cheap. I still want to maximize value when I make purchases, but now it isn't only the price that I consider. I consider quality, longevity, functionality, and so on. And yes, some things we buy now are nicer, name brand, and a step above what we bought in the past.

If you had a million dollars today, what would you do with it?

We would likely split that up and invest at least half of it, put another portion into short-term savings to be used for something bigger that we would normally save for, keep some to use immediately on needs like minor household repairs, wardrobe updates, etc., and some portion to use freely for anything we want, including giving some of it away.

Can the keeper become too comfortable? What does keeper complacency look like?

I don't think the keeper becomes too comfortable, but the identity could be underdeveloped in the beginning or fade later, causing poor behaviors to come back. The entire process involves reflection and intention. This is not a set it and forget it lifestyle. We either control our lives with intention or someone or something else will.

What's the difference between a keeper and a sage? How do you know you're transitioning?

I think it's when you begin to think in terms of contribution rather than return on investment. Asking yourself what will help others grow instead of what will help me grow. Considering what will cause positive change long after you'll be around to observe it. It makes me think of that Benjamin Franklin example of leaving money to Boston and Philadelphia. He knew he would not see the future value benefits of that gift in his lifetime.

If warrior danger is burnout, what's keeper danger?

I think the biggest danger with the keeper identity is moving too fast and trying to force it. That won't work. It takes time and purpose, and without them it will be a constant challenge to let the warrior truly rest.

Part 3: Relationship Patterns & Personal History

Looking back, how did warrior identity affect your relationships, not just with money, but with people?

It was impossible to be social and have friends that I stayed active with. There was just never enough time. It also prevented me from pursuing some hobbies that I genuinely love doing, like playing guitar, foraging mushrooms, and hiking.

The constant motion and vigilance shows up in marriage as sacrificing time and experiences for work and making money.

Was your wife in warrior mode too? Or was she keeper while you were warrior?

I don't think she was in warrior mode herself but was in warrior-support mode. This is an important thing for a partner to understand about themselves and to know how their significant other is operating.

What did your wife do that helped you become keeper? What didn't help?

There wasn't anything specific that she did that helped identify or help with the transition to the keeper role, but she was always there to support whatever I was going through, so that kind of emotional safety net certainly helped with the process. What didn't help? We may have slightly different perspectives on discretionary spending now that the debt is gone. HA!

Did your kids repeat your financial patterns, or did they avoid them because they saw the cost?

I think most young adults operate within the warrior identity for a time simply because it's a big leap from being supported by your parents to operating as a self-sufficient adult. I don't think any of them are repeating the same patterns that I did, but they also didn't come from the same place I did. I just hope they're able to see these identities in themselves and turn that recognition into something meaningful.

What did you try to teach them about money? Did they listen?

They constantly heard about budgeting, emergency funds, and the dangers of credit cards and debt. I think they've gone through the typical arc where kids hear the lessons from their parents, but don't engage in it right away. It's not quite real to them at first, but with a little life experience and reflection, I think they understand why I tried to teach them those things. I wish I had put more emphasis on time margin, but that's not something I could hide from them so it would have felt hypocritical. Still, I did everything I could to be present in their lives, and I hope they felt that growing up. I still maintain an active presence in their lives, and that brings me a very deep level of joy. I'm proud of them!

Part 4: The Transition Process

How much of your transition was chosen versus forced? Would you have left healthcare management without the layoff?

I was already planning to leave healthcare; I was just offered an opportunity to do it ahead of schedule. So, I guess you could say it was chosen as a plan but forced in its timeline.

What about readers who won't get laid off with severance? How do they transition without that external push?

Well don't forget, the severance and other financial payouts didn't end my debt, it only accelerated the payoff. The transition starts with recognition, which I didn't have words for at the time. I didn't have a way to recognize any of these identities in advance. It took a major shift in my life before these patterns came into focus for me. That's the entire purpose of this book, to give others language and words for what they may not understand about themselves and hopefully use that to be intentional about these changes, rather than understanding through circumstances and hindsight as I did.

Is it possible to leave the warrior identity while still employed? Or does crisis always catalyze change?

I think crisis is often a catalyst for change, but not a healthy one. A person can absolutely leave warrior mode while still employed once they're able to recognize that's the identity they're operating in and that it may no longer be suitable for their needs and goals. I mean, I was employed the entire time before, during, and after identifying these themes and going through them.

You had a five-year plan to leave healthcare. Would you have followed it, or did the layoff just accelerate something already in motion?

We were already in the process of following that plan. The layoff only changed the timeline, nothing more in that regard.

What would you tell someone in peak warrior mode who wants to transition but has no crisis forcing them?

I would tell them to do some deep internal searching and reflect on whether the warrior identity is still necessary and if it is moving them toward a better, healthier life, or just sustaining something that's familiar. I would tell them to complete the self-assessment I've provided here. Once you have the tools, you don't need to face a crisis to start working on this.

Part 5: Practical Details

Why was the college willing to hire you so quickly for the full-time teaching position?

The number of classes I had already taught and the number of years I had been teaching were the biggest factors. It also helped that I shared many of their teaching styles, like using real world examples to demonstrate concepts, using project work instead of boring homework, and adding things, like creating a personal budget, that gives students useful tools as well as developing Excel skills. I'm sure it helped that I sort of fell out of the sky just in time for them to avoid cancelling classes and losing revenue!

Do you still work for the same college?

No, I worked there for two years and then was offered a teaching opportunity at another local school that perfectly aligns with my interests in economics and finance. The university I work for now is one that I taught at as an adjunct for six years before joining the full-time faculty. It's an excellent fit and I'm very happy and grateful for how it all worked out.

Looking back, was teaching at seven institutions as an adjunct "desperate overwork" or was it building something?

I was definitely building something, I just didn't realize it at the time. What an incredible outcome! I had no idea at the time where all that teaching experience would lead me, but that "desperate overwork" paid way more dividends than just extra income.

How did your financial advising practice start? What was your first client like?

I was approached by an MBA classmate not long after graduating. I was not very skilled at the time, but I believe what I provided them was valuable. Years later I would hear from them that the recommendations I made were still serving them well and that it helped them change their course.

Why is your practice referral-only?

It's simple keeper boundary-setting. I don't have the time to build a business, and it's not what I want to do as a major activity in my life. I may not even continue with it down the road, but it gives me some practical experience and exposure to real situations people face, so it is beneficial for my other work as well.

What do you actually do in your advising practice? How many clients do you typically work with?

It's a fee-based business. I provide a full financial review with recommendations in any area I see improvement opportunity. I also provide an Excel-based budget for them to use if they choose to do so and help them get started with it. I encourage them to utilize any kind of budget over none at all, so whether they use mine or not isn't as important as just using one.

I rarely have more than three or four clients at any given time. I don't maintain an office outside of my home because it's just unnecessary overhead, so I typically meet with clients in their home or another location if they prefer.

When did it stop feeling weird to advise people while you were still carrying debt?

I think it stopped feeling weird before we were debt-free. There was a point when I knew I was providing practical and valuable advice that was not related to my personal situation. Just like I mentioned before, a doctor with cancer can still treat someone with cancer.

Is financial advising keeper work, or sage work?

Probably keeper since it helps build the foundation of knowledge in that space and contributes somewhat to my research interest. It may become sage work through things like this book and other writing I hope to publish that may help a larger group of people who aren't necessarily my clients.

Part 6: The Book Itself

Why did you write this book? Was it financial? Contribution? Both?

100% contribution. If I can give someone the tools and insight to recognize these patterns proactively instead of retroactively as I did, then this will all be worthwhile.

Is publishing this book an act of sage identity?

I think it has sage components. I hope if the book truly helps someone that they will give it to someone else who needs it. I want this to help people I will never meet.

Are you trying to build a platform for your financial advising practice, or something else?

It's not for me. I would like to think that the financial counseling field may consider the need for post-poverty and post-debt identity crisis care. I think there is a gap beyond what the spreadsheet shows as financial crisis that needs to be addressed. This will be the primary focus of my doctoral research.

How will you know if this book succeeded?

If I hear that it changed just one person's life, I will consider that to be success.

Final Thoughts

What's one final thought you'd like readers
to keep?

The people who told me I couldn't do it, that
I'd never make it. The versions of myself I've
left behind. The expectations and burdens I
carried that were never mine to begin with.
The scarcity that shaped me but no longer
defines me. The fight that no longer has an
opponent.

I don't carry those things anymore. I'm done
bleeding for ghosts.

And if you've made it this far, if you've
recognized yourself in these pages, in these
patterns, in this framework, then maybe
you're ready to stop bleeding for your ghosts
too.

You don't need a crisis to start. You just
need to recognize where you are and decide
where you want to be. Decide *who* you want
to be.

The rest is just time, intention, and the
courage to let the warrior finally rest.

Acknowledgements

This book exists because people believed in it before I did.

My wife, Shannon, deserves more credit than a single paragraph can hold. She lived through nearly every version of the story told in these pages, through the accumulation, the crisis, the transition, and the slow work of becoming something different. She never asked me to be the keeper before I was ready, but she made space for him when he started to emerge. Her patience, support, and willingness to let me figure this out at my own pace made everything else possible.

My children, Forrest, Vanessa, and Cassidy, who didn't choose to be part of this story but were with me through it all. You saw the warrior up close, the constant motion, the divided attention, the exhaustion I tried to hide but couldn't. Your childhood was shaped by a cycle I was desperately trying to keep from reaching you. And my bonus children, Jordan and Jenna, who would only learn later where my story began, but witnessed the peak of it all. I hope the keeper is a better father than the warrior was. Thank you for your patience while I learned the difference. My life wasn't complete until all of you were in it.

To Joana Ramsey, Barb McDonald, Kevin Klein, and RJ Podeschi who believed in me and who were instrumental in helping me find the greatest and most rewarding career I could have imagined. You opened doors I wouldn't have knocked on without your guidance and encouragement. And Jan Kirby, Diana Heeb Bivona, Kristine Mantey, Jonathan Pierce, Kelly Munson Smith, Vance Laine, Michael Harden, Mark Munoz, and Salem Boumediene who gave me so many opportunities to build this career I love and become the educator I am today.

To the many colleagues I met through nursing, IT, leadership, and teaching who became my friends during the hardest years, you know who you are. The ones who checked in after my world changed suddenly, and the ones who continue to check in today. And my fellow "five-percenters" who have thrived in their personal and professional lives following a major career disruption. I'm blessed to share this space with you.

To my former and current professors, many of whom are now colleagues who have provided me with so much support and insight. You are truly the best of the best.

To my students: You asked questions I didn't know I needed to answer. Your struggles with money, identity, and the pressure to perform became the lens through which I finally understood my own patterns. This book started in those conversations, in the margins of finance and economics lectures, when you trusted me enough to admit you didn't have it figured out either.

To my early readers: Your feedback shaped this book in ways I couldn't have managed on my own. You pointed out the gaps, challenged the assumptions, and asked the questions that made the framework stronger. This work is better because you cared enough to be honest.

And finally, to everyone who's ever felt like the warrior, running faster, working harder, carrying more, and wondering why it never feels like enough. To those who have lived through poverty, whether you've escaped or are still trying. To those who have been caught in the debt and lifestyle trap. This book is for you. Not because I have all the answers, but because I've been there and still am some days. The keeper takes time. Be patient with yourself. The work is worth it.

About the Author

Jason "Jay" Sexton is a college professor teaching finance and economics, and a financial advisor specializing in the behavioral and philosophical aspects of money management. He is pursuing a PhD in Personal Financial Planning at Kansas State University, where he is a member of The Honor Society of Phi Kappa Phi.

His journey from poverty to professional success, and the identity crisis that followed, became the foundation for the warrior-keeper-sage framework presented in Bleeding for Ghosts. After spending over thirty years operating in what he calls "warrior mode", surviving through constant motion, accumulation, and vigilance, Jay experienced the disorienting transition to a more sustainable way of living. His research now focuses on post-poverty and post-debt identity crisis, exploring the psychological and behavioral shifts required when survival and escape are no longer the necessary modes of operation.

Jay lives in Illinois with his wife and family. When he's not teaching or working with clients, he's hiking, reading, cooking gourmet food, and spending time with his grandkids. He's probably also updating the budget. Bleeding for Ghosts is his first book.

For more information or to connect with Jay, visit https://www.sextonfinance.com or on LinkedIn at https://www.linkedin.com/in/jasonwsexton/

Discussion Questions

1. Jay describes three identities: warrior, keeper, and sage. Which identity do you see most active in your own life right now? What evidence supports that assessment?

2. The book argues that the warrior identity often forms in response to scarcity or crisis. What shaped your relationship with money, work, and rest? Can you identify the origins of your own patterns?

3. Jay experiences a "post-debt identity crisis" after becoming debt-free. Have you ever achieved a major goal only to feel lost afterward? How did you navigate that transition?

4. The concept of "voluntary sacrifice" is central to the keeper identity. What's one thing you could sacrifice voluntarily now to build margin for your future self?

5. Jay describes margin as distinct from minimalism. How do you understand that difference? Where do you fall on that spectrum?

6. The warrior often shows up differently in different life domains, like work, health, relationships, rest. Where is the warrior most active in your life? Where have you successfully transitioned to keeper? Do you see sage work in any part of your life?

7. The book emphasizes that the keeper may take years to develop, not months. How does that timeline shift your expectations for your own transition?

8. Jay discusses the danger of "post-debt drift", relaxing boundaries once the crisis passes. Have you experienced this pattern? How did you respond?

9. The sage identity is presented as aspirational and difficult to reach. Do you know anyone who embodies sage characteristics? What makes them different from warrior or keeper?

10. If you could have a conversation with your past self at peak warrior, what would you want them to know? What wisdom would you share?

11. Jay writes that "the warrior knows how to fight, but the keeper has to learn how to live". What does learning how to live, not just survive, look like for you?

12. At the end of the book, Jay states, "I'm done bleeding for ghosts." What are your ghosts? What would it mean to stop bleeding for them?